13 STEPS
TO
A MORE DYNAMIC PERSONALITY

13 STEPS
TO
A MORE DYNAMIC PERSONALITY

Carl G. Goeller

and

William O. Uraneck

Parker Publishing Company, Inc.

West Nyack, New York

Printed in the United States of America
ISBN-0-13-918417-1
B & P

To my father, the late Carl Goeller, Sr.
—a very dynamic person.

CG

Thirteen Steps to a Dynamic Personality

Something is going to happen to you as you read this book—something dramatic and exciting! Whether it happens after reading the first or 13th chapter isn't important. It *will* happen! And once it does, your life will never be quite the same again!

This is no exaggeration; it's a fact! We know it will happen because we've been there when it's happened before—Bill Uraneck as a leading consultant in industry and a teacher in both college and industry, and Carl Goeller as an editor, business executive, and teacher of creative writers and artists. Many hundreds of times in our professional careers during which we've trained and developed people to make full use of their talents and abilities, we've seen it happen.

We've seen men who've stayed put in the same job for years suddenly move up the ladder as a direct result of their re discovered powers. We've seen people who were bored with life suddenly become active, dynamic people who eagerly look forward to each new day. We've seen writers, artists, engineers, teachers, executives, office people, salesmen, clerks, people in all walks of life, bring their native talent to the forefront and become dynamic forces within their fields. We've seen men and women double and triple their incomes as a direct result of their new-found personalities. We've seen manufacturers increase their volume and profits dramatically through new ideas and new methods resulting from these techniques. We've seen people improve their relationships with others; seen them use their supervisory skills more effectively; seen them improve their home life, family life, and love life dramatically. We've seen "ordinary" people accomplish things they never even dreamed possible before.

During recent years we've also seen top management of industry and business become increasingly aware of the necessity of having creative, dynamic men and women within their organizations. Today, more than ever before, they need such people. They need their problem-solving abilities and quick, alert minds; they need their creative talents and good ideas. And today they're doing more than just talking about the need for dynamic people: they're seeking them out, and paying for them—paying well!

THIRTEEN STEPS

Each of the 13 chapters of this book provides you with a step toward greater use of your creative powers and the development of your dynamic personality. With the help of these 13 "keys" you will enter into a new phase of your life—a phase in which you become the kind of productive person you were intended to be. Take them one at a time. Examine them, then use them! They will help you to accomplish many things:

To tap your *brainpower* for an unlimited number of *ideas*.
To achieve the necessary *enthusiasm* to sustain your dynamic personality.
To *solve problems*, large and small, successfully and *creatively*.
To make *greater use of your time*, thus increasing your accomplishments.
To *generate ideas* and to spark idea creation in other people.
To develop an all-round *dynamic personality*—the 24-hour-a-day kind.
To *increase your income*.
To *become more successful* in your chosen field.
To *sell your ideas*—and yourself.
To more effectively *supervise* and *teach* others.

To have a *more dynamic marital and personal life.*

To learn how to *enjoy living* and get more out of life.

To make the *change* a *permanent* one through *forming good "thinking" habits.*

YOU HAVE A PRICELESS TREASURE—USE IT!

The greatest gift this human race of ours has ever received is our brain; and perhaps the greatest tragedy in the infrequency with which we use it. Scientists tell us that we use *less than 10%* of its available powers!

If you had a bank account which contained a billion dollars, payable on demand any time, and place, would you consent yourself with drawing $5 or $10 a week from it for the rest of your life? Of course not! You would draw on it often and freely, putting it to work for you to do those many things you've always wanted to accomplish, to help you live the kind of life you've always wanted to live.

What a terrible waste it would be to let that kind of fortune sit virtually untouched and inactive throughout your entire lifetime! Yet it happens every day to millions of people. They barely tap or ignore altogether their greatest treasure—their brain! It's impossible to exaggerate the wonders of your brain—that storehouse of limitless amounts of information, creator of limitless numbers of ideas, and control center of your entire personality. Did you know, for example, that with some 60 billion memory cells your brain is capable, during your lifetime, of storing 50 times more information than is contained in the entire Library of Congress?

To match the brain's remarkable memory storage and computing power would require a machine the size of a 150-story building which would need an entire city of people to maintain and operate! It would cost more billions of dollars than any space program to date; and it would still be unable to produce one single creative idea! Don't waste your magnificent reservoir of ideas by making simple "$5 and $10 withdrawals" from it. Program it well and draw upon it often. There are quick, effective ways to do this —and we'll discuss them in our early chapters.

STEPS TO ACTION

Once you've started drawing upon your brainpower for ideas and solutions to problems, you will want to put them to work for you—profitably, in your job, your business, and other income-producing ventures. We will show you, with some down-to-earth basic principles and through dozens of case histories, ways in which you can achieve success and financial gain. We'll show you many simple yet effective approaches up the ladder to success.

STEPS TO PERSONAL SATISFACTION

We purposely did not stop with a how-to-succeed-in-business approach to this book, because being a dynamic, creative person is a round-the-clock proposition. Once you turn on your imagination and idea power, you won't be able to turn it off. You'll find your dynamic personality playing a key role in all facets of your life—in relationships with your family, friends, the opposite sex, and even your enemies. You'll find it influences your moral and religious philosophy as well. This book is intended to awaken you to *all* the satisfying ways in which your newly-developed dynamic personality can enrich your life.

EXPERIENCE—THE BEST TEACHER

Through the book we've used many case histories (there are nearly 300 in all) to illustrate points and methods. We've selected these particular incidents from files containing over three thousand such cases. You'll find no Churchills, Einsteins, Henry Fords, or Hemingways in these case histories—only "everyday people" from all walks of life. We did this to prove that creative minds and dynamic personalities are not the exclusive property of statesmen, genuiuses, or famous artists. The principles we demonstrate in this book work for everybody—regardless of background or level of formal education.

ALL YOU NEED IS YOU—THE *REAL* YOU

You'll discover amazing things about the development of your dynamic personality—that bringing it to the surface actually requires so little you don't need costly equipment. There are no special courses to take. All that's necessary is for *you, yourself*—using *your* own time, talent, and abilities—to simply unlock something that's been there inside you all along—*the real you!*

NOW LET'S GET STARTED!

There are exciting and rewarding times ahead of you as you read this book, so let's get started. Plan to read at a steady pace, a little each day, so you can receive the full benefit of its cumulative effect. Don't hesitate to backtrack and re-read those chapters and passages which pertain most directly to you. And be sure to put the principles outlined into effect immediately. Don't wait for some mystical "right moment"; do it now! Remember:

Today is the very first day of the rest of your life!

Carl Goeller
William O. Uraneck

ACKNOWLEDGMENTS

In a book in which nearly 300 case histories are cited, an accurate list of credits would seem endless, but there are those special people whose encouragement and help contributed greatly to the gathering of material and the writing of this book, and to them I am deeply indebted: My wife, Kay—my creative partner and very valuable critic; Irving Stone, president of American Greetings and one of the most dynamic personalities in the business world today; and my creative team of associates who spent many hours reviewing, criticizing, offering invaluable suggestions on the manuscript itself, and helping in its preparation: Casey Beregi, Doris Bidwell, Doris Faulhaber, Betsy Gerus, Colleen Gutta, Carolyn Herrmann, Mac McGuire, Pat McCorkle, Jean McManus, Lucy Mills, Dorothy Monahan, Maureen Monroe, and my daughter Sheila. A special note of thanks to The Christophers and their dynamic founder, Father James Keller, for the use of several of the case histories in these chapters.

Carl Goeller

Much credit is due to Alex Osborn, founder of the Creative Education Foundation and leader of the annual Creative Education Institutes held in Buffalo for the past 16 years, and to Dr. Sidney J. Parnes and Dr. Lee H. Bristol, Jr., who took up the reins of leadership after Alex died. My wife Liz and my daughters Nancy, Dotti, and Diana spent many busy hours cranking out articles and stories on the home mimeograph, and to them I owe a great deal. Also, to professor Edward McGee and Dean Frank Genovese of Babson Institute, who supported a graduate course in Creative Thinking for years; my personal friends, Don Madden, Jack Kennedy (Ohio), and Jim Proctor, who have always come up with good ideas when needed; and the many students who shared with me their personal experiences in creativity. Without such people this book could never have been written. I can't help but give full credit to Carl Goeller because one day, a couple of years ago, he asked, "Why don't we write a book about our favorite subject?" —which we did.

William O. Uraneck

Table of Contents

—Often It Is • Respect Time—But Don't Worship It • 100 Ideas for Making Time Work for You

Creative Power Tools • Your Dynamic Power Source • Dynamic Calculators • The Idea Analyzer • The Idea Selector • Now Take Care of It

Your Dynamic Personality Training Calendar

Ideas That Make Money • Ideas That Build Image • Ideas for Pleasure • Ideas That Provide a Service • Ideas That Enhance People's Personal Power • Ideas for Increasing Your Income

Creativity • Craftsmanship • Consideration • Confidence • Ideas for a More Successful You

Ten Ways to Sell Your Ideas • Ideas for Selling Your Ideas

When You Teach, Be Imaginative • Learn the Principles of Dynamic Teaching • Be Dedicated • Communicate on a Me-to-You Basis • Try New Methods,

1

"Turning On" Your Mind . . . and Watching the Ideas Come!

Thinking is the hardest work of all . . . that's why so few of us do it!

Henry Ford

The snarling holdup man motioned impatiently with his ugly revolver toward the two frightened janitors, indicating they were to climb into the trunks of the shiny sedan floor models on the automobile showroom. "Please," the older cleaning man pleaded, "don't make us crawl in there!" "Y-yeah," stammered the other, "we won't call the cops, honest!" "I'm not taking any chances," the burglar growled, "Get in! It's only a few hours till morning and someone will let you out then."

Still protesting, the men crawled into their respective luggage compartments. The thief slammed the deck lids and gave a satisfied nod as each locked firmly into place.

By morning, when the trunks were finally opened, one janitor had nearly died of suffocation and was rushed, unconscious and in critical condition, to the hospital. The other was badly frightened, but still alive and healthy. How had he survived?

He had made life-saving use of the air in the spare tire. Each time he was nearly out of breath, he took a whiff of air from the spare. Quick thinking had saved his life. There was a spare in the other trunk, too, but the man there had apparently not thought about using it.

Ideas are a lot like the air around us—invisible and sometimes elusive, yet essential to our survival. Like air, ideas are available almost any time and in any quantity. If you learn to harness them properly you can unlock your mind and become a more valuable, dynamic person than you ever dreamed you could be.

And that's the primary purpose of this book—to help you ventilate your mind and let the clean, fresh, invigorating air of new ideas rush in to stir up excitement, adventure and accomplishment. It's intended to help you turn on your dynamic, creative personality!

How do you "turn on" your dynamic personality? And *why* should you in the first place?

In this book the authors will help you to answer the first question —but only *you* can answer the second one. So do it now!

Do it right now—before you read another page. Decide why and in just what ways you want to be more dynamic and creative. What do you want to accomplish in the near future? In the more distant future?

Get a pencil and copy the checklist below on tne left side of a sheet of paper. Divide the right side of the paper into three vertical columns. Head the first: "Definitely want to do!" Head the second: "Interested," and the last column: "Not for me." Now, in each column check those goals towards which you sincerely want to make real progress. Don't skip over the list with the idea of coming back to it later. Check it now so you will have your goals visibly in mind; then apply the ideas and techniques, which will be revealed throughout the book, to achieve those goals. Fold the paper and keep it with this page.

Goals

A.   1. To become better in my field
      2. To move ahead in my field
      3. To become tops in my field
      4. To make more money
      5. To make a *lot* of money

B.   6. To achieve self-satisfaction
      7. To gain recognition
      8. To find new interests
      9. To add excitement to life
     10. To be more appealing to the opposite sex

C. 11. To solve problems more easily
   12. To become better organized
   13. To make better use of my time

D. 14. To have more friends
   15. To be a better spouse
   16. To raise my family better
   17. To become a better person
   18. To be a more interesting person

E. 19. To help other people
   20. To better serve a cause in which I believe
   21. To make my life count for something worthwhile

F. 22. Other goals (list them)

As you move through the book, study the principles outlined and the case histories shown and ask yourself, "How does this relate to me—and to the goals I checked?" Keep your goal-ideas relationship in mind at all times. Each time you pick up the book to continue your reading, turn to your list and review your goals. With these goals in mind, your reading will become more meaningful.

100 IDEAS A DAY!

Did you know that the human brain is capable of creating 100 or more ideas every day? How many have you come up with today? Yesterday? If you're "average" the answer will be two or three! And there are many persons who never reach that figure. Sad, isn't it, when we read that the average person uses less than 10% of his brain's creative potential! What a goldmine must be hidden in our untapped 90%! Let's think about it for a moment.

Imagine what would happen to you on your job—or at home—or at the next social event you attend—or in your love life—or in your adult-child relationships—or for that matter, in *anything* you undertake, if you were to raise that total of two or three good ideas a day to five or six or ten—or more? It doesn't take much projection to determine that your life would never be the same again—and neither would you! You *can* accomplish this. The tools to do so are available to you right now. Develop them properly and use them well and often and you'll find they become easier to use and more effective every time you do use them.

Let's take inventory of the tools you'll be using:

1. A *storehouse* of experience or "memories" in that built-in computer, *your mind.*
2. The *imagination* to play with these memories and combine them into ideas.
3. A *dynamic personality*—the kind which will enable you to project and communicate your ideas.

For a quick, down-to-earth example of how these three things work towards the creation of good ideas, let's take five common things from another *storehouse*—your cupboard. We'll need a glass, a toothpick, an olive, a bottle of gin, and a bottle of vermouth. By themselves they comprise five usable but not very exciting items. Through some *imagination* in combining these five items, however, you will eventually come up with a martini—something much more exciting! Finally, your *dynamic personality* will determine how you might present your martini and to whom.

Selecting the right time, place, and person or persons is vitally important to the ultimate enjoyment of your martini! Do you get the picture?

Then we're ready to start, by answering these questions: How do you collect memories? How do you store them? How do you combine them with imagination?

Ideas Are Like Air

Let's return to the analogy between ideas and air and discover how you can harness ideas from the creative atmosphere around you. Borrowing Junior's basic science book, we find there are four ways in which man converts air into power:

1. He harnesses *moving air*—by capturing it with windmills, sails, etc., and converting it to power.
2. He uses *air pressure*—employing air to help move something heavier than air, as in the instance of sipping a soda through a straw.
3. He *compresses air*—containing and compressing large

quantities of air and releasing it in small but powerful doses.

4. He relies on *air resistance*—for example, using air to break the fall of a parachute.

Relate this now to the methods available to you for gathering your thoughts, information and memories, and converting them to ideas.

Use Your Mind Like a Windmill

Like a windmill drawing power from the moving air around it, use your mind actively to collect ideas from everywhere, then start your thought processes to working. Strive for quantity first and let the subsequent chain reaction of creative energy help you toward solutions.

Be curious—stop, look, listen . . . and ask questions.

Be alert—don't let the world pass you by. Discover where the action is, then go there to gather ideas.

Be consistent—make idea-gathering a full-time project. Keep paper and pencil handy all the time so you can jot down ideas as they come . . . wherever you may be.

Play around with ideas—don't just file them away. Start combining them and applying them to problems at hand. Turn old ideas into new ideas, little ideas into large ones.

To observe the "windmill" approach in action, look at the case history of Howard Landis.

Howard, because of family financial problems, didn't complete high school. An early marriage forced him to take a routine, low-paying job in a large corporation. He was not well-liked by his supervisors because he was "nosy" and had a maddening habit of asking "why?" about every task he was assigned. Rather than simply doing the job, he delved into the routine, challenging its very existence, questioning the thinking that led to the assignment —often even the system itself. He would not move on a project until he was completely sure just how it could be handled most effectively and efficiently.

At lunchtime Howard would seek the company of people in

other areas, asking them questions about their jobs, the firm's product, its market and anything else about which he was curious.

His supervisor, growing weary of endless explanations of *how, why, when* and *what if,* gave him less and less to do. To fill the resulting time gaps, Howard began using the information he'd gathered at lunchtime, playing with new ideas and inventions relating to the firm's product. When the boss discovered this, he became furious, but since the ideas had been developed on company time, agreed to present them to the creative development department. The ideas were well-received and the department requested Howard's transfer to their area.

Today Howard is a key man in the company's creative development program at an excellent salary. His strong curiosity, restlessness and desire to experiment helped him overcome his educational deficiencies.

Use a "Soda Straw"

There are times when the windmill method is too broad and too general in the information it produces. There will be times when your problem is a very specific one and you need to get down to the nitty-gritty quickly. When this happens, it's time to make use of air pressure—use your mind like a soda straw. Find, or make, a "soda" of information or possible solutions to a specific problem, then draw from it, filling yourself with ideas and digesting them to your satisfaction.

Suppose, for example, you are a small restaurant owner and you want to expand your menu to include Oriental dishes, but your knowledge of Oriental foods is very slight. There are several approaches you might take:

Study up on your subject. Read everything you can find that's been written on the subject—cookbooks, magazine articles, newspaper columns.

Talk to people who are knowledgeable on the subject and get their ideas. Discuss their successes and their failures. Talk with friends or neighbors who cook Oriental food; talk with restaurant people; if your time and budget permit, travel to some Oriental countries and discuss cooking methods with "ordinary" people as well as professionals.

Experiment. Try dozens of different recipes and approaches. Discard those you don't like, keep those you do. Try different seasonings and different cooking methods until you are convinced you've hit "the" combination. Watch others experiment. Profit by their experiences.

Use what you've learned. Don't be satisfied with simply being a theorist. Do it—and do it often. Experience will always be the best teacher, and the more you cook Oriental food, the better you will become at cooking Oriental food.

Expand your range of interests. It's good to be a specialist, but it's better still to have a variety of interests in addition. Here's an example in the case history of the remarkable Paul Brewster—a man who has made extensive use of "soda straws" to improve his home and his surroundings:

Paul uses his imagination in everything he undertakes. He has no formal training in architecture, engineering, biology, or any of the "mechanical" fields. When he wants to learn how to do something, he goes to libraries and reads up on his subject. He studies books, magazines, reports, and finished examples of the items under survey. Then he completes his education by doing. His creative accomplishments include the successful completion of these home projects: Designed and built his own home; worked out the details of plumbing, electricity, carpentry; built out of waterproof plywood a portable Japanese bathtub which accommodates two adults and three children; built a summer guest house without using any plans—simply working out problems of design and construction as he worked on the building; designed and built his own greenhouse; designed and built his own furniture; for a hobby, makes pottery—builds the kilns, the wheels, and experiments with native clays and native grit to make exotic finishes. For his wife's nursery school he has designed and built outdoor swings, ladders, slings, playhouses, monkey houses, and other recreational devices. Then, just for the fun of it, he built a two-man submarine, doing all the design work, fabrication, setting the controls, power unit, navigational instrumentation, periscope—the works. It worked, too! Here is a man who is imaginative with his hands and fingers, even though he can only moderately express himself verbally or in writing.

Keep a Parachute Handy

Minds are like parachutes: they only function when they're open. In order to *have* ideas you must be *receptive* to ideas, and to do that you must keep an open mind all the time. Luck is a major factor in creating things but you can often make your own luck by capitalizing on what's going on around you. Open your mind like a parachute in order to take full advantage of the circumstances and ideas that surround you. Here are some ways to keep your mind open and active:

Broaden your interests. Go new places, see new things, meet new people—do something new every day!

Stay alert. Notice what's going on around you; read new books and magazines. Snoop; what are people saying? How can all this relate to your goals and problems?

Capitalize on events as they happen. Learn to recognize opportunity by its knock and open the door quickly. Don't be afraid to speak up—and don't let false modesty slow you down.

Widen your circle of friends and acquaintances. Make sure they know your abilities, goals and dreams. Don't be a recluse; be where the action is and you're more likely to get a piece of the action.

Put "luck" to work for you. Think of yourself as lucky— believe it! Luck needn't always be something that happens to the other guy.

Observe how Massachusetts engineer, John Loren, combined his broad field of interests with a special assignment to turn a hobby into a major part of his job:

John Loren had several hobbies, one of which was rifle shooting. His friends knew about it and so did his employers. Thus, when his company received an order which they were not "programmed" to handle—that of building a set of controls for a rifle range—they handed the project to John. He and his crew examined all of the nearby rifle and pistol ranges and came up with several improvements over existing ranges. They were well-received. Within three months, John's company was installing control systems not only for police departments but for jails as well. John investigated moving targets and learned that there were very few competitors in this field, so he began working on target-making, too. He learned that the Armed Forces use millions of plywood targets for which they pay well, but which they soon discard because they splinter quickly. He developed a target which does not splinter and lasts ten times longer. He also developed new items such as target systems that are self-scoring and targets for shooting galleries which "shoot back" at the person firing. What began as a special assignment now constitutes a major part of his job. Being in the right place at the right time with his imagination has paid off handsomely.

Use an "Airhammer" on Tough Problems

Tough problems often require tough, concentrated methods. Just as scientists can take all the air in a room and compress it into a few small cylinders to operate powerful pneumatic drills, so you can compress ideas gleaned from experience, study, and brainstorming into an airhammer approach to any problem. This approach requires filling your mind with dozens, sometimes hundreds, of bits of information and ideas on a given topic, then being able to throw them out again in a steady stream as they're needed. Many times you'll find it necessary to gather the thoughts and ideas of others through brainstorming or bull sessions. An example of the compressed air approach is this classic story of the American naval vessel in enemy waters:

> The ship, a battleship, had moved into a bay on an outgoing tide and suddenly found itself stuck snugly in the mud, unable to move. There was nothing to do but sit tight until the tide returned early in the morning. Nothing, that is, until the lookout shouted, "Floating mine heading directly toward the ship!" The huge mine with its ugly porcupine-like stickers covering the surface was so close to the ship that it was impossible to shoot and explode it without doing serious harm to the ship. In less than three minutes, the mine would contact the ship's hull and explode.
> The ship's officers quickly brainstormed possible courses of action, but none seemed practical. Finally it was a suggestion from

an alert ensign that the captain put into action. He ordered the firehoses to the side of the deck and streams of water trained on the floating mine. The intense pressure of the water was successful in pushing the mine a few feet beyond the bow, and the relieved crew watched it float harmlessly away.

IMAGINATION . . . THE PRICELESS INGREDIENT

Have you noticed that all of the approaches to idea collecting and development thus far have one very important thing in common? They all require more than just collecting ideas—they require *imagination!*

In northern Ohio an underground river feeds into a pond called The Blue Hole. This river pumps enough water from beneath the earth to provide a complete water supply for a town of 70,000 persons. But as it is, it's worthless. It contains no oxygen, thus can sustain no life. It is useless for fish or any other living creature until it passes through a series of water-wheels which mix oxygen into the water. So it is with our collection of information and memories. Unless we mix our imagination with them, we haven't given "life" to any ideas.

In subsequent chapters we'll discuss specific ways you can turn on your imagination to accomplish those things you really *want* to accomplish (remember your list of goals?) We'll cover practical, proven ways in which you can become a more dynamic, creative person. For the moment, however, let's recap this chapter by looking at a publishing executive's definition of a dynamic person.

What Is a Dynamic Person?

Look around you at the office, the store, the neighborhood, the home or anywhere else you happen to be, for the most enthusiastic, most creative, the happiest person you can find—and you'll see a dynamic person.

A dynamic person is versatile, has many moods and talents. He refuses to tie his mind down to a single idea, project, thought or philosophy for very long. He stays loose; enjoys juggling many projects at the same time. The more complex the problem, the more fun there is in solving it. He avoids ruts as though they were graves. He's the man at the desk, doodling on a pad of paper—or the fellow at the outdoor grill trying a new recipe—the pressman who takes his wife to see a play by Shakespeare—the accountant who goes on a camping trip with his family—or the housewife who's shouting "Kill the umpire!" at a ball game.

A dynamic person is a curious person. He wants to know the "Why?" to everything, whether or not it's any of his business. He wants to know how it's made, what it's made of, who made it —and what makes it run. He collects facts as some people collect stamps or calories. He can never get enough. He wants to learn about new fields and areas of interest, to read new articles or books, to watch or listen to new programs. He enjoys learning new skills, meeting new people and seeing new places. He's willing to try anything—at least once.

He STOPS—when he feels he's moving through life too fast to take the time to become a more dynamic, interesting person. He stops to watch a sunset or a beautiful cloud formation or to read a bit of history on a roadside marker or to help someone solve a problem. He stops, but only to recharge his batteries. He refuses to procrastinate.

He LOOKS—to the right and left as well as straight ahead. He realizes that his vision is limited only by his ability to keep his eyes open. He looks at a painting to see what the artist is trying to tell him. He looks at those around him to see what he might learn from them.

He LISTENS—to those older and wiser than he so he may profit from their hard-earned experience. He listens to the young because from them he can find truths so obvious the adult world might overlook them forever. He listens to impractical dreamers, to super salesmen, to the angry, the hurt, and especially the lonely. He listens to his relatives, his friends, his spouse—and even his in-laws. He listens to the dull and ignorant, for as the philosopher said, "They, too, have their story to tell."

A dynamic person is a restless person. There are a million things his fertile mind has dreamed up for him to accomplish and he knows he's going to have to hustle to get them all done. Given a choice, he would rather have time than money—because he knows it's far more valuable.

He likes to play with ideas—sometimes with a definite purpose in mind, sometimes just for the heck of it. While he likes to see his ideas come to fruition, he may well get more enjoyment from just playing with them. He likes to juggle, re-arrange, combine, delete, stack, knock down, throw, catch, submerge, cut in half, tack together or paint over. He's as interested in failures as in successes because from them he's gained some knowledge too.

A dynamic person approaches with a childlike simplicity. He is enthusiastic about every new thing he approaches. He can't afford the sophistication of blocking or rejecting ideas. He attacks new problems and ideas with no holds barred and is willing to get down on his hands and knees and touch, feel, taste, bounce, and inspect them himself instead of letting others relate reports wrapped in their limitations and prejudices. His mind is always open, whether to the door-to-door salesman, the sidewalk philosopher, the humbug—or his favorite person of all, a young child.

A dynamic person is an independent person. He doesn't always play by the same rules. In this world of "let's belong" he likes to be alone sometimes. He enjoys people (and they, him) but he never really becomes a part of the crowd. He'll forsake a good poker game or golf match or even an "important" meeting to simply "go thinking" somewhere away from the rush and crush of routine.

He is independent but not unreasonable. He respects the opinions of others, but he chooses his projects and directions without any really serious concern about those opinions. He knows that if "they" were running the world, very little would ever be invented.

A dynamic person is confident of his ability to solve problems and achieve goals. He frequently sticks his neck out.

A dynamic person is imaginative and inventive. There is a tremendous thrill in creating something new—or helping someone else create it—and he wants to taste that thrill regularly. He enjoys solving problems with improvised methods and tools or adapting whatever is on hand to do the job.

A dynamic person is a dedicated person. He thoroughly likes his work, his life, his surroundings, and he will spend great amounts of time, energy, and resources to make it an extension of himself. He is an expert in his favorite field and he works hard to maintain this position.

A dynamic person establishes goals, values, and ideas as early as possible. He first learns to believe in himself, then in his ideas and his affiliations. He is intense about everything, but especially about his family, his neighborhood, his friends, his country, his religion.

A dynamic person sets priorities. He realizes he can't do everything at once, so he schedules himself and those who work for and around him to do first things first. He isn't a clockwatcher, but he treats time with the great respect it deserves.

A dynamic person is stubborn. He refuses to give up on an idea or a goal. If he feels its time has come, he'll move heaven and earth and nearly everyone around him to convince them of its worth. If he realizes, however, that its time hasn't come, he will put it on ice for a few months—or years—but he never gives up.

A dynamic person is an interesting person. He is fun to talk with because he has more to discuss than the weather, the latest soap operas, how many miles he has traveled this week, or how his wife doesn't understand him. He is fun to be around because his enthusiasm is contagious. He is fun to work with, or for, because he makes it all seem purposeful and worthwhile.

Look around you and you'll see that you're surrounded by dynamic people, although many of them haven't discovered the fact yet.

Now, step over and look into the mirror. Do you see the very dynamic person who is staring so intently at you? Strange coincidence, isn't it? *A dynamic person is someone like you!*

RATE YOURSELF

Score yourself as a dynamic person. How do you rank in each of the traits just mentioned: versatility, curiosity, restlessness, simplicity, independence, confidence, imagination, inventiveness, dedication, goal-orientation, ability to set priorities, interest to others? Rate yourself now, before you move onto the next chapter. A month from today, come back and rate yourself again. Where have you improved? Where do you need still greater improvement? Have you lost any ground? Now, mark your calendar so that a year from today you'll come back and rate yourself once again. Your rating should be from 1 to 100%. A 100% ranking would mean you're doing the very best you possibly can—practically perfect. A 90% would mean you're close to the top in your field on that particular point. 50% would be "just average"—and so on.

If you've given yourself a 60 or below on any category, then that should be the starting point for your improvement campaign. Begin with your low ratings and work twice as hard to bring them up. Even where you've scored a 90 or better, give it that little extra push to get yourself up to the 100 mark. Above all, don't let low marks discourage you. Rather, let them be a challenge to you —then rise to meet that challenge!

2

Putting Your Imagination to Work Solving Problems

There is no problem of human nature which is insolvable.

Ralph Bunche

The pessimist claims life is just one problem after another. The optimist says life is a long series of opportunities. Actually, *both* statements are true! Problems *are* part of life—a daily part—but every problem in need of solving presents a new opportunity for you to grow and develop creatively. It's to your advantage, then, as a dynamic person, to become an efficient problem solver.

It often looks easier than it is. In the world of television, life's problems are solved quickly and easily. A lifetime accumulation of psychological hang-ups can be remedied completely in a one-hour show; the problems of social acceptance are solved handily in 30-second commercials by simply using the sponsor's products. Switch to different aftershaves, toothpastes, deodorants, or cigarettes and POOF!—like magic, your problems disappear!

Unfortunately, real life is seldom that simple. Yesterday's problems are still today's problems regardless of the soap you use or the car you drive. And you need solutions for them! There's no such thing as magic—the puff-of-smoke type, anyway—but there are some very magic words you can use to solve your problems and to turn them into opportunities.

Skeptical? Then try them! Properly used, any or all of the following magic phrases can enable you to spot, isolate and solve even the peskiest problem. Look the list over—perhaps you've used some of the phrases lately. Decide which can best help you solve your present list of problems.

"This is a problem—and I am going to work on it!"

To solve any problem you must first know what it is. Pinpoint it, isolate it, and you're ready to solve it.

"I refuse to let this problem dampen my enthusiasm!"

Sure it's a tough problem, most of them are. But problems are not solved by defeated, negative thoughts. You need a full head of enthusiasm and positive thinking to sustain your creative efforts. Keep smiling! Keep trying!

"I will tackle this problem now—before it gets out of hand!"

Like that loud noise in the motor of your car, most problems won't vanish by being ignored. The sooner you solve a problem, the less damage it will have accomplished in the meantime.

"If I can't handle it myself, I'll ask for help!"

Draw upon the experience and memory stockpiles of others, too. Ask for help when you need it. Profit by the creative efforts of those who've faced similar problems. If two heads are better than one, then three heads are better than two—and so on.

"I want to understand all facets of the problem!"

Like an octopus, a problem may have many troublesome features. Be aware of all of them and don't give up on a problem until you've neutralized them all. An octopus with one tentacle gone is still a dangerous customer!

"I will not confuse the apparent problem with the real problem!"

You can waste precious time and creative energy attempting to solve the wrong problem. Study it carefully and make sure you understand the real problem before you spring into action.

"I will solve this problem creatively!"

The first solution that comes to mind may well cause more problems than it solves. Brainstorm the problem: tackle it from many angles before reaching your solution.

"I intend to turn this problem into an opportunity!"

Look to the future with your solution. Let it be a springboard to a new adventure—or your next creative solution!

Sometimes a single one of these magic phrases will start you towards a solution. Other times it may take two or three—or perhaps all of them before you strike pay dirt. Look at the bag of "magic" engineer Wayne Richards went through before finally solving a knotty problem:

Wayne, a native New Englander, had been placed in charge of a manufacturing plant in Virginia. To provide the thousands of gallons of water the plant needed daily, it was necessary to accumulate a reservoir of some eight million gallons adjacent to the company's property. This required the purchase of four acres of farmland near the plant, but when Wayne approached the owners, he found them unwilling to sell.

"This is a problem and I am going to solve it."

He increased his offer, but to no avail. Next, he tried to exert some friendly pressure through a local realtor, but this nearly backfired and threatened to turn the owners' coolness into potential hostility.

"I refuse to let this problem dampen my enthusiasm."

After the owners refused another monetary offer, Wayne decided to work around the reservoir and complete the rest of the plant in hopes that the farmers might have a change of heart and sell later. The reverse happened. The townspeople began growing cold on the whole project and some of the young people even began harassing the building operations.

"I will tackle the problem now, before it gets out of hand."

He decided to petition the local town council for intercession in his behalf with the owners.

"I'll ask for help."

Before doing this, however, he asked the foreman, a native of the area, for advice on how to best approach the council.

"I will not confuse the apparent problem with the real problem."

The foreman said that Wayne was barking up the wrong tree and would probably never be able to force the landowners to do something they saw no reason to do. They didn't need the money, so there was really nothing in it for them. "You just haven't offered them anything interesting yet," he concluded.

"I want to understand all facets of the problem."

Re-evaluating and re-defining his problem, Wayne concluded that his solution lay not in forcing them to sell, but rather in convincing the farmers that the reservoir could be as attractive to them as it was necessary to him.

"I will solve this problem creatively."

A five-minute brainstorm session with his plant foreman provided the solution.

"Now, I will turn the problem into an opportunity."

The next day, Wayne approached the owners of the farm, but instead of making a forceful New England-type approach, talked to them about everything but the reservoir. The conversation seemed to be heading nowhere when he casually said, "If I build the reservoir here, I plan to stock it with catfish and allow all local residents and plant employees to fish in it." The catfish did the trick. All resistance vanished, and the owners couldn't do enough to expedite the project. In addition, farmers and workers from miles around applied at the employment office for work at the plant in order to enjoy the coveted "fishing privileges."

This Is a Problem and I Am Going to Work on It!

Notice, though, before any of the other magic phrases can be called into play, the first, *"This is a problem and I am going to work on it,"* must be stated—and believed. This is the magic key that will activate the rest. You can solve any problem once you are aware that you have one!

I Refuse to Let This Problem Dampen My Enthusiasm

If at first, you don't succeed—you're running about average! One of the quickest ways NOT to solve a problem is to let a few dead ends cause you to say, "To heck with it!" You can lighten a weighty problem when you brighten up and smile. There is more power to a punch delivered in high spirits than one delivered in low spirits. Remember, too, to solve a problem you have to *want* to solve it—and when you're feeling down and out, it's hard to want to do much of anything. Each failure, mistake, or dead end is simply a friendly invitation to keep trying!

> Probably no one knew this better than Thomas Edison who, to find a substitute for lead in the manufacture of storage batteries, conducted some 20,000 unsuccessful experiments. A reporter asked him, "Aren't you discouraged by all this waste of time, effort and materials?"
>
> "Waste?" Edison shot back. "Nothing is wasted. I've found 20,000 things that don't work!"

I Will Tackle This Problem Now—Before It Gets Out of Hand

Scarlet O'Hara of *Gone With the Wind* had a simple system of solving her problems—that of saying, "I'll think about that tomorrow!" The trouble with that philosophy is that there is an infinite number of tomorrows and an official "problem-solving day" never arrives. Twentieth century problems have an aggravating way of growing when they're neglected long enough, so it's vital to tackle them as soon as you can.

One example of a problem in which time is a definite factor is cigarette smoking. The Cancer Society tells us that every cigarette a person smokes can shorten his or her life, and that every cigarette a smoker lights up serves to entrench the habit more firmly. It's appropriate, then, that a timepiece figured both literally and symbolically in the following example of creative problem solving:

A West-Coast doctor, himself a chain smoker, read a scientific report which said that the habit of smoking is related to certain times of the day—mealtimes, breaktime, commuting to and from work, or any time a cup of coffee is available. He reasoned that if the habit of associating smoking with these particular times could be broken, the hold on the smoker would be much less— and quitting much easier.

So he developed a timing device with a miniature alarm system, pre-set to go off at random times during a day. Smokers are given the devices and instructed to smoke only when the buzzer sounds, regardless of the time of day or what they are doing. It may buzz during a meal, in the midst of a project, during a walk, any time —but when it does the smoker must light up. He is not allowed to smoke any other time.

Soon the habit of smoking at specific times during the day is broken and the "victim" looks forward to the next buzz rather than to the next cup of coffee. The alarms are set by the doctor to ring with less and less frequency each week until finally the smoker is down to one or two cigarettes a day. At that state, a complete withdrawal becomes relatively easy.

The doctor reports that there is considerably less back-sliding among smokers using this method because the old tempters (meals, coffee breaks, etc.) are no longer associated with lighting up a cigarette.

If I Can't Handle It Myself, I'll Ask for Help

"No man is an island," said John Donne, and his statement rings as true today as in 1630. We can't expect to accomplish everything ourselves. We need the help, encouragement, and ideas of others. Don't be afraid or ashamed to ask for help. First, it will sincerely flatter the recipient of your request that you consider his opinion worthwhile, and second, he just might have some darned good ideas to help you solve your problems. Look at the help these "experts" received from youngsters:

"Why don't you ask the kids themselves?" suggested the wife of a young Massachusetts architect when he confided that he and his partner were having difficulty with a suitable design for a new elementary school. So that's what the two men did.

A few mornings later, the architects met with some 80 third, fifth, and seventh grade pupils and brainstormed with them.

"Think," said one partner, "what kinds of materials, shapes and textures do you like in school? How do you feel about split-level homes or schools? How would you like a shopping center type school with classrooms along an arcade?"

The answers and ideas came quickly, including "Why can't we have classrooms like the teachers' lounges or the rooms we have at home?" One fifth grader suggested classrooms on a merry-go-round with pushbuttons for teachers to ask the children questions. Nearly all the students liked the shopping center approach. Armed with comments, the two men soon presented preliminary sketches and proposals to parents and teachers for a unique design much like a shopping center with learning centers clustered in strategic corners of the split-level building. As a direct result of one child's suggestion, there were bridges to allow the children to use the nearby town hall, health center and library for learning purposes.

Not all the ideas were accepted, of course. The children will have to do without wall-to-wall carpeting and merry-go-round classrooms with pushbuttons—at least for the present.

I Want to Understand All Facets of the Problem

It's no secret that problems beget problems and before long you can end up grappling with a Hydra (remember the monster from Greek mythology that had nine heads—and grew two new heads for each one cut off?). Explore all possibilities before you even attempt to come up with your solutions; otherwise, you could be chopping off one head and watching two more grow back. Look what almost happened in this incident from industry:

Kent Crossen, a production executive for a hardware manufacturer, was an extremely competent engineer but he was also considered unreasonable, impatient and demanding by his fellow executives. Things came to a head concerning Kent over the purchase of some new equipment which he had recommended as a substantial cost-saver. The purchase was approved but as time went on and equipment was not installed, Kent began hounding his boss (a vice president), the head of purchasing and the production manager, to get in the equipment. Finally, after the purchasing director called Kent's boss and demanded he keep Kent physically away from his area, the vice president went to the president and recommended that Kent be asked to resign. He explained that the headstrong engineer was a problem which would infect the entire company and cause dissension among the rest of the executives.

The president called Kent to his office. "These things take time," he explained to Kent. "Why?" was Kent's response. The president had no answer to that, so he began checking. He found that:

1. Every month the new equipment wasn't in operation, it was costing the company $6,000 in labor.
2. Two of the company's competitors had already installed the equipment—to his company's disadvantage.
3. The purchasing delay was unnecessary. No shopping was required since only one firm made the equipment.
4. Paul's apparent "unreasonableness" was based on frustration rather than obstinacy.

The president called a meeting of his top men at which he told them their problem wasn't Kent—it was the speed at which the company was used to operating. He accused his people of dragging their feet with no one pushing to see that things got done in a hurry. To correct the problem, he set tight time limits on all future projects. He charged his executives with establishing a new tempo throughout all their operations.

The company began to develop spirit. Employees and departments who had previously dragged their feet now competed with each other to speed up operations. The spirit of achievement filtered down from top management to office, plant and sales personnel. Because the president took the trouble to see what the problem was with his "problem child," Kent, the whole attitude and direction of the company was changed—for the better.

I Will Not Confuse the Apparent Problem with the Real Problem

Problems, like icebergs, aren't always completely visible, and you may often find yourself attempting to solve what *looks* like the problem and completely overlooking the *real* problem—the one lurking beneath the surface. Naturally you should try to solve a problem as quickly as possible before it gets out of hand, but there is a real danger in rushing into a solution before you're certain you know the problem. Take a look at this example:

> Troubled by the increasing highway accident and death toll, especially on the turnpike, the State of Florida authorized a commission study of other state safety campaigns. In its report the commission pointed to the efforts of a neighboring state which had had an extensive campaign underway to control speeding on the turnpikes and other high-speed highways. This included radar, unmarked patrol cars, and even the use of helicopters and light aircraft to catch speeders. The efforts were impressive, but the results were not. In spite of the increased arrests, accidents and fatalities continued at virtually the same rate as before.
>
> The "why" to this seeming paradox was pointed out in a medical report which said that the problem was not so much speed as fatigue, which was a far greater cause of accidents than speed. Drivers, lulled almost to sleep by long monotonous stretches of effortless driving, tended to be less alert to sudden dangers, more prone to dozing and loss of control. The real problem, the commission concluded, was how to reduce driver fatigue on turnpikes. A proposed solution, both creative and unique, was adopted by the Florida turnpike: Install free car washes! The idea was to lure motorists into service plazas for "something free," which would give them an extra opportunity to relax and stretch their legs, thus making their journey safer.

I Will Solve This Problem Creatively

Keep in mind there is a big difference between solving a problem and "creative problem solving." The truly creative solution is one whereby you not only remedy the immediate problem but also set up some future chain reaction which can lift you to a new level of creative activity. For a light-hearted example of this, take the problem of Pete the poet:

> Pete's wife was tired of watching her husband's rejection slips pour in as fast as the bills and pressured him almost daily to give up his writing and "go to work." One day she delivered an ultimatum—if he didn't get something published within the next 60

days, he would have to decide between writing and a wife. He agreed and extracted a promise from her that if he *did* get published—even once—she would not nag him again about his writing. "In fact," he added, "I'm going right to the top: I'm going to be published in the New York Times!" With evident skepticism, she agreed to abide by this. The enterprising young man then wrote a letter to the "action-line" column of the Times which said:

> Can you or any of your readers give the words to the poem which begins,
> "In the still of a cloudy night. . . "?
> Also, may I have the author's name?

This was published. Then he wrote a letter (signed and mailed by a friend) which gave the poem in full, along with the author's name. Thus the writer had his poem published in the Times, satisfying his ego and silencing his wife. (Incidentally, he was published legitimately a few months later.)

I Intend to Turn This Problem into an Opportunity

Here's a true test of your dynamic personality! If you can develop the ability to turn any problem, from the smallest irritation to the greatest disaster, into a worthwhile opportunity, there will be no limit to your accomplishments. If you're a student of history, you can name dozens of generals who won battles but lost wars because they contented themselves with solving the problem at hand—usually the capture of a city or a country—and failed to capitalize on the opportunity for a complete victory which presented itself at the moment. But this doesn't just happen on the field of battle; it happens all around us every day. The average person, having solved the problem at hand, tends to smile with satisfaction and say, "Well, that's that—a job well done!" As a dynamic person, though, you mustn't allow yourself to be content so quickly and easily. Complicate things a little; be ready with questions that must be answered before you go on to the next problem. Ask questions that can open new doors and new opportunities —questions like these:

How else can I use this idea?
Can I use my solution to solve someone else's problem?

Will this method work on unrelated problems?
What will happen if I keep on going?
What if I make this temporary action permanent?
Is the timing right to use this on a larger scale?
How much is my solution worth? To whom?

Emergencies father hundreds of good ideas which solve immediate problems and then go on to become permanent additions to our cultural or business world. Here's a contemporary example:

In Minnesota, the telephone company had a problem: gophers were chewing on underground cables, eventually severing them and disrupting service. The company requested help from a nearby chemical firm which responded by concocting an evil-tasting brew which was then incorporated into the polyethylene jackets around the cables. It was successful—the gophers hated it!

Their assignment was completed and the chemical people could have rested on their laurels, but they didn't. They asked themselves, "How else can we use this idea?" and began investigating other uses for the unique concoction. An alert marketing man recalled reading about problems the Army was having in Vietnam with jungle rats gnawing through helicopter power cables, and he suggested the firm contact the Defense Department. Tests were run using the process on the helicopter cables. The results were satisfactory and the chemical company received a healthy government contract as a result. Now the firm is investigating uses for the formula in computers, commercial aircraft, and other commercial devices.

Sometimes extraordinary solutions can lead to some interesting and unique opportunities. For an example, see how three Louisville real estate developers converted some gigantic white elephants into a whole new concept of apartment dwellings:

The businessmen bought a large milling plant from a major flour manufacturer. It included 24 deserted 98-foot-high silos which the men planned to tear down. They thought they would, that is, until they were presented with the cost. It was cheaper to leave the structures standing vacant than to destroy them. But it was also a terrible waste of valuable space as well as being a civic eyesore.

They brainstormed numerous solutions before one of the trio

suggested turning the silos into apartment dwellings for young singles. He cited recent reports of California's flourishing colonies for the young and unattached which stated that next to being in each other's company, nothing appeals to young singles as much as doing something different. The partners agreed that silo living would be different, indeed! They contacted an imaginative architect who concluded that the silos could be converted into 12-story apartment buildings, and well within the budget the businessmen had in mind. In addition to being different, the building had the attraction of being close to the center of town and proved to be an instant success. Now the developers are considering other "kooky" types of apartments in other cities.

It was Alexander Graham Bell who said, "When one door closes, another opens, but we often look so long and so regretfully upon the closed door that we do not see the one which has opened for us." And this brings us to a very important point. *Don't let panic, the pressure of time, or the opinion of others force you into an unsatisfactory compromise to your problem.* This is a sure way to miss the golden opportunity that may be awaiting you when you reach a good solution or make a right decision. Be confident in your ability and look for the new door which has opened for you.

Paul and Thomas, both members of middle management, lost their jobs when their employer, a manufacturing firm, ran into financial problems. At that particular time the job market was poor, and both men had no luck finding positions similar to their previous ones. Finally Thomas panicked. The house payment was due, expenses were piling up and his family was worried, so he took the nearest job he could find—that of a shoe salesman. "It's just temporary," he told himself.

Paul was in the same financial bind but he refused to give in to worry. He told himself that this immediate problem wasn't necessarily to get a job—it was simply to earn enough money to support his family. So he contacted several small firms—one within his own industry, and others in related fields—and offered his specialized knowledge on a consultant basis. The firms, all too small to afford the full-time services of a person with his skills, were pleased to obtain such services for a nominal amount. Paul soon had more clients than he could handle, so he recruited help. He now has an active management consultant firm going and his income is double that of his former job.

Thomas is still selling shoes and complaining bitterly to anyone who will listen about the dirty deal life has dealt him.

The next time you face a problem, analyze it thoroughly, solve it creatively, then start asking yourself the key questions that will turn your problem into a greater opportunity than you dreamed existed!

USE YOUR MAGIC PHRASES OFTEN— AND EFFECTIVELY

Will these eight magic phrases mean a problem-free life for you from here on? Let's hope not! Because even though problems can be irritating, troublesome, frustrating, annoying, and disrupting, you would be in bad shape without them!

That's not as paradoxical as it may sound. Let's face it—as long as you have goals to accomplish, you're going to have problems waiting to block or divert your accomplishment. If you had no problems, it would mean you had no goals—or at least none worth the effort. And it's an established fact that goals and objectives are literally lifesavers. The medical experts agree that when you have a reason for living you are going to live longer than those for whom life no longer represents a challenge. The challenge of problems and the satisfaction that comes from meeting them head-on and solving them effectively contribute enormously to the excitement of living.

If you feel your job lacks this kind of challenge, then seek it elsewhere. Tackle problems within your professional organizations, social activities, your church, your marriage, your hobby, in politics—any place in your circle of living where you can put your creative powers to work. Remember, as long as you have something to look forward to, your mind will respond with creative enthusiasm—and that's the stuff upon which a dynamic personality thrives!

YOUR GOALS—AND YOUR PROBLEMS

Turn back to the place where you have put a paper listing your goals, and select what you consider your primary and secondary goals. Copy them on the left side of another sheet of paper, and divide the right side into two columns, one headed "Problems I Face" and the other "Best Magic Solution Starters." Now, in the second column, list the present problems facing you which could prevent the immediate achievement of these goals. Then in the third column, list one or more of the "magic phrases" of problem solving which you feel would be most useful in helping you solve these problems.

Once you've done this, you're well on your way toward that elusive solution. Then repeat the procedure with the next two goals on your list—and so on.

3

Throwing Away Your Mental Crutches

The brain has muscles for thinking as the legs have muscles for walking. Without frequent exercise, those muscles will deteriorate.

J.D. de la Mettrie, 1748

It isn't always easy to be a dynamic person—to think positively and creatively and to solve the problems that face you. There will always be those who are quick to say "It can't be done!" They'll have some pretty convincing "reasons" too.

These "reasons," though, are seldom more than crutches—mental crutches—intended to help you take the easy way out of problems and challenges. And mental crutches are dangerous! Almost without your realizing it, they can keep your brain limping along and your performance far below your potential. Their end result is sevenfold:

> They prevent creative thinking.
> They make ruts all too comfortable.
> They stifle new ideas.
> They prevent constructive activity.
> They dull the senses.
> They cripple ambition.
> They destroy self-confidence.

Learn to spot them, understand their function, and then deal accordingly with them. Your dynamic personality may often depend on your ability to lock up your crutches.

To help you recognize the many different varieties of crutches, we've arranged a short "tour" for you through a mythical factory which we'll call the American Crutch Corporation. The company is fictitious, of course, but the crutches are real—very real.

Ready? Let's go.

"Come in, folks, come in—and welcome to the American Crutch Corporation. We're the largest and most successful manufacturers of crutches in the world and our specialty is MENTAL CRUTCHES—guaranteed to be the most reliable anywhere!

"American Crutches have been manufactured for centuries, but it hasn't been until the 20th century that their usefulness, reliability and comfort were discovered, and perhaps not until the last 30 years or so that mental crutches really became a major factor in the American way of life. Today, according to reliable sources, nearly 98% of our population uses our crutches! Isn't that astounding? How many other products can claim that kind of universal appeal?

"Now, please notice the area to your left, the one with all the file cabinets. This is where we produce our ever-popular BUSINESS WORLD CRUTCHES. With the advent of the large corporation, the demand for crutches for the business world has increased at a fantastic rate—some tenfold during the last two decades alone. There was a brief period of apprehension on the part of our marketing people that the increase of computers might well end the need by industry for crutches, but fortunately, the opposite has been the case.

"These files contain every known mental crutch used, to date, in offices, factories and stores around the nation. Many of you will doubtless recognize some of our more popular models. Perhaps you even use some of them yourselves. But for your convenience, we've labeled each. In case you can't see them from where you are, I'll list them aloud for you:

"Our all-time best-seller is WE'VE ALWAYS DONE IT THIS WAY—easily applicable to every type of business situation.

"Running a close second are two old standbys—WE TRIED IT ONCE AND IT DIDN'T WORK and IT WOULD COST TOO MUCH!

"Many businessmen tend to favor our newer models, such as LET'S FORM A COMMITTEE TO STUDY IT; THE BOSS HAS A PERSONAL

PREJUDICE AGAINST THAT; IT'S A GOOD LONG-RANGE IDEA, BUT WE NEED SOMETHING MORE PRACTICAL NOW; and WE HAVEN'T THE EQUIPMENT FOR THAT KIND OF JOB. These all tend to have a nice professional ring to them.

"You may recognize some of our other models as merely streamlined versions of older crutches. They include WE JUST BARELY HAVE TIME FOR THE NECESSARY WORK (in the old days, this was called WE'LL HAVE TO TRY THAT WHEN WE HAVE SOME SPARE TIME); THAT'S NOT MY JOB; IF IT DOESN'T WORK, WE'LL ALL BE FIRED; and THAT CALLS FOR A MANAGEMENT DECISION.

"And here are some newer models which show promise of becoming future staples: THAT'S SOMETHING THE COMPUTER CAN HANDLE BETTER THAN WE CAN; THE COMPUTER DID IT—IT MUST BE RIGHT! WE'LL CONSIDER IT WHEN WE DO NEXT YEAR'S BUDGET; and BEFORE WE PROCEED FURTHER, WE'LL NEED MORE MONEY!"

Amusing? Perhaps, but not very funny because crutches such as these can inhibit the growth of any company as well as most of the individuals within that company, oftentimes for years. Take for example these two firms in the same industry—one which used many mental crutches and another which refused to allow them. The results speak for themselves:

Ten years ago a New England manufacturer of greeting cards and paper products, grossed some 35 million dollars. The organization had just emerged from a disastrous period in its life during which a series of wrong decisions at management level had cost it dearly in sales volume, lost dealers, and internal talent. Once out of the woods, management adopted a "safe" course in marketing and manufacturing. A modest sales goal was set each year and a stringent budget established. At this point, mental crutches came into the picture thick and fast—crutches such as NO EXPERIMENTING—ONLY TESTED IDEAS and IF IT'S NOT IN THE BUDGET, FORGET IT! Middle management became conservative and used still more crutches, like SAVE THAT IDEA FOR WHEN WE CAN AFFORD IT; IT'S NEVER BEEN DONE—LET COMPETITION TEST THAT ONE FOR US; and IF IT FAILS, YOU'LL DO THE EXPLAINING TO THE BOARD OF DIRECTORS. The employees began using crutches such as WHY BOTHER—IT'S MANAGEMENT'S PROBLEM; THE COMPANY DOESN'T CARE ABOUT ME, SO WHY SHOULD I CARE ABOUT IT and I KNEW IT WAS WRONG BUT IT WASN'T MY WORRY! This year the company grossed a little over 50 million but was in serious trouble. Its stock reached its lowest ebb; profits were down; and the firm has lost dozens of its most creative people as well as competent members of management and middle management.

Another greeting card publisher, located in the Midwest, grossed just over 40 million dollars ten years ago. The firm's dynamic president refused to permit crutches within his organization. He was far from satisfied with the company's performance and set himself and his people a sales goal of 100 million dollars within five years. In pursuing this goal, he and his management team became chronic crutch-breakers. Attempts to use crutches like IT'S ALWAYS BEEN DONE THIS WAY were repulsed with THEN IT'S TIME WE CHANGED IT! To the crutch WE'RE NOT IN THAT FIELD he would counter THEN LET'S GET INTO IT. A WE DON'T HAVE THE MACHINERY crutch would be shattered by THEN FIND SOMEONE WHO DOES AND WORK WITH THEM! His daily greeting to his creative staff was "WHAT'S NEW?" When they had no reply he demanded reasons. He set up suggestion boxes throughout the office and plant areas and paid thousands of dollars yearly for ideas and money-saving suggestions from his employees. Middle management seldom had time even to consider crutches. They were too busy exploring new ideas and experimenting with new procedures and streamlining outdated methods. Whenever someone tried to use an IT CAN'T BE DONE crutch, he would be met with TELL THAT TO MR. S. (the president). The company reached its hundred million mark on schedule and today is hard at work on its new goal of two hundred million.

On a more personal basis, mental crutches can weaken many a dynamic personality.

A dynamic personality with a creative solution to a problem makes a strong combination.

Now let's proceed to the next station on our mythical tour where our guide will acquaint you with some widely used crutches that can easily cripple the dynamic personality.

"Our next stop is where we make convenient PERSONALITY CRUTCHES. Most of these are mid-twentieth century specials and have resulted in reducing the lives of millions of people to deadly routine and almost unbelievable boredom. Glance over our complete stock; you'll recognize many of them, I'm sure.

"Our most universal models are I SIMPLY DON'T HAVE THE TIME; I'M TOO TIRED—I NEED TO REST MY BRAIN, NOT USE IT; WHAT WOULD PEOPLE THINK? and I'LL HOLD OFF TILL THE KIDS ARE RAISED AND GONE.

"Next in popularity and still very effective are WAIT TILL WE CAN AFFORD IT; WE'LL SEE HOW THINGS ARE NEXT WEEK (a bestseller, by the way); THERE'S A GOOD PROGRAM ON TV; IT'LL WAIT; I'LL DO IT LATER; IT'S TOO WILD—I'D FEEL SELF-CONSCIOUS and I'VE NEVER TRIED IT BUT I'M SURE I WOULDN'T LIKE IT.

"Other especially convenient crutches are: I CAN'T; I DON'T KNOW HOW; I HAVE TOO MANY FAMILY OBLIGATIONS; I HAVE ENOUGH TO DO WITHOUT TAKING ON ANYTHING NEW; and, of course, those all-purpose crutches DON'T ROCK THE BOAT and I'M SATISFIED WITH THINGS JUST AS THEY ARE!"

Our enthusiastic tour guide neglected to mention something important (for the dynamic person, not himself). There are numerous crutches which can cause us to live our entire lives in a comfortable rut—but *all* of them are breakable! They break easily when exposed to the creative efforts of a dynamic person. There are dozens of keys to neutralizing these personality crutches. Here are a few of them:

> Trying a new idea on your job
> Surprising your boss, your spouse or your best friend
> Eating a new food or cooking a new way
> Dressing a new way
> Going out to see something new
> Going someplace new to you
> Reading a book outside your field
> Talking to a stranger
> Helping the new person in the office

Like any key, however, they only work if you *use* them. Put them to work often!

BEWARE OF HABIT-FORMING CRUTCHES!

Nearly all mental crutches can become habit forming, but this holds especially true with those you'll see at the next station in our mythical tour.

"Now, folks, this department features ALL-PURPOSE CRUTCHES. While many people prefer to specialize, some can use the same crutches at work or home, or when they are socializing, or for any and all occasions! Note the timeless versatility of these crutches like THIS JUST ISN'T MY DAY; OH, WHAT'S THE USE!; I'VE

BEEN SICK; I DON'T HAVE TIME; and I'VE NEVER HAD A CHANCE! With a little imagination, you could get by an entire lifetime just on these few crutches, and never even have to draw from our larger stock. The beauty of these crutches is that they place the blame on 'fate' and excuse the user from any further form of positive accomplishment, whether he's at the office, out golfing, driving the car, or working around the house. It relieves him of the burden of doing anything constructive for the balance of the day—sometimes longer!"

The way to overcome these crutches is simply to refuse to accept things as they are. When trouble hits, fight back and keep trying no matter how often you lose. If you aren't satisfied with your lot in life, change it—don't just complain about it. One of the symptoms of a dynamic mind is taking adversity and turning it into something positive or useful, as in the case of this creative housewife:

> Her husband accidentally overturned and broke her favorite blue glass vase. She couldn't bear to part with it, even in a shattered state, so she carefully collected the pieces. Her hobby was making leaded glass pieces for hanging in windows. She sold many of these at a gift shop near the beach. Looking at the shattered vase, she had the idea of using the pieces as sails for a stained glass sailboat, thus giving her work a three-dimensional effect. Her sailboats were an instant hit and she soon had more orders than she had broken pieces—so she purchased another vase and had her husband break it. From that time on, all her glass items used the 3D feature, selling for much more than the ordinary kind. Creative thinking and determination offset an OH, WHAT'S THE USE crutch.

I DON'T HAVE THE TIME is another all-purpose crutch frequently used for postponing mental improvement for days, weeks, years— or even a lifetime. It is a universal fallacy that there simply isn't enough time in a 24-hour day to get things done. As we'll discuss in the next chapter, if one really wants to accomplish something, he will *make* the time. Here is a case in point:

> Dwight O'Neill began inauspiciously enough by dropping out of school at the age of 16, then joining the army for four years. There were many crutches waiting for him upon discharge—

crutches like I'VE NEVER HAD A CHANCE; I'VE ALREADY WASTED THE BEST YEARS OF MY LIFE; THE ARMY TOOK ALL THE FIGHT OUT OF ME —but Dwight was determined to make up for lost time. He completed high school in 90 days, then raced through college in three years while supporting a wife and family by working eight hours a night in a service station. While in graduate school he learned about electronics by reading every issue of two prominent scientific journals covering a 20-year period. To "round out" his education, he checked out a book a day from the library and stayed up each night until he had completed reading it. He continued this practice for 20 years. He is now a prominent electronics scientist.

ALWAYS TRY THE OBVIOUS FIRST

We often make our own complications by reaching all around for solutions that were right under our noses all the time. Our tour guide has an appropriate name for such situations. Let's listen:

"In the far corner of our Research and Development department are several pilot models of an item we call a NOSESTRETCHER. The purpose of a NOSESTRETCHER is to enlarge one's nose to such a degree that the wearer is no longer able to see right under his very nose and thus discover some obvious answers to problems."

There are cases, of course, where nosestretchers aren't necessary. Many people just naturally fail to see the obvious. They insist on attempting complicated solutions, thus becoming perfect prospects for crutches such as I'VE TRIED EVERYTHING; IT CAN'T BE DONE; and THE SOLUTION WOULD CAUSE MORE TROUBLE THAN THE PROBLEM. Here is a typical case in point:

A photographer for a publishing firm was angry and frustrated because people kept bursting into his darkroom as he was developing pictures, thus ruining the film by exposing it to sudden light. He posted DO NOT OPEN signs on the door; he moved the darkroom to a less-trafficked end of the building, but the parade of intruders continued. He placed furniture in front of the door to make entry more difficult—and still people barged in. Finally he asked an office boy to stand guard in front of the door during such times as he was developing. For this service, he was willing to pay out of his own pocket, but the stockboy replied, "Why don't you just lock the door from the inside?" The embarrassed photographer gasped—he hadn't thought of that!

A similar "difficult" problem was solved by a simple suggestion from advice columnist Ann Landers in a recent column. The writer, a distraught wife, had this story to tell:

> We have only one car, so each day I must drive my husband to work—and it's wrecking our marriage. No matter how carefully I drive my husband criticizes me. I'm either going too fast or too slow or I don't see this car or that one. Honestly, by the time I get him to work, I'm a nervous wreck and he's in a foul mood. He says it's making him nervous and irritable at work, too. What can I do? I need a car during the daytime.
>
> Miss Landers went directly under the writer's nose. She said simply: Let your husband drive to work and you sit in the passenger seat. Once he leaves the car, then you drive it home.

Each time you fail to start your search for a solution right under your nose, you are a candidate for one or more crutches. Always start with the obvious.

DON'T MAKE CRUTCHES A HABIT

Few people are really aware of the deterioration in their mental muscles caused by mental crutches. Like anything comfortable, mental crutches can become a habit and a permanent part of your mentality. When this happens, creative thinking and dynamic action become impossible simply because you will no longer consider them necessary. In short, you will have become so used to your pain you feel no urgency in treating or curing it. See what happened in this case history:

> Ed Baker, one of the most creative men in his company, was given the responsibility of developing ideas for new products. He tackled the job in a great burst of enthusiasm and energy and put in many overtime hours experimenting and designing new items. Initially the company used many of his ideas; however, a budget slash soon resulted in management's accepting fewer and fewer ideas. After a meeting during which *all* of his latest creations had been rejected, Ed began using one of the oldest crutches

—THIS COMPANY DOESN'T REALLY WANT TO TRY ANYTHING NEW! From that time on, his approach was more perfunctory than creative. His ideas became merely slight modifications of ideas he had presented earlier or which the company had already tried. As his acceptance rate dropped to rock bottom, he began using another crutch: THOSE STUPID JERKS WOULDN'T RECOGNIZE A GOOD IDEA IF IT BIT THEM! One day management accepted a clever idea from a youngster in another department—an idea unique in its simplicity, yet clever enough to capture the public's fancy. Ed's crutch I COULD HAVE DONE THAT IF THEY'D TOLD ME WHAT THEY WANTED carried him through the next few weeks—right up to his termination. Had he not relied so strongly on crutches, he might have recognized that management's *real* problem was budget and they liked the young man's idea because it was inexpensive as well as creative. In short, the deterioration caused by his use of crutches cost Ed his job.

DREAM—BUT DO IT DYNAMICALLY

Some crutches appear to be quite creative at first—*daydreaming*, for example. It's important to learn how to distinguish between creative daydreaming and crutch daydreaming. Perhaps our "tour guide" can throw some additional light on this distinction.

"Another important group in our R&D area are our DREAM DUST designers. Theirs is the responsibility of developing new, improved methods for making people permanent daydreamers—permanent to the point that they never accomplish anything beyond daydreaming. There are some fine crutches available for daydreamers—crutches like SOMEDAY I'M GOING TO DO SOMETHING ABOUT THAT; THIS ISN'T WHAT I REALLY WANT TO DO FOR THE REST OF MY LIFE; IF I COULD ONLY GET AWAY FROM IT ALL; and THEY'D HAVE A DARNED HARD TIME OF IT IF I WERE TO LEAVE!

"The object of these crutches is, of course, to keep people in a perpetual dream world—to hang creativity on the 'someday' hook and never bring it back down to earth. DREAM DUST must be handled carefully, naturally, because dreaming is also an essential part of creative thinking—at first. It becomes the task of Mental Crutches to help people use dreams as *escape* from reality rather than as vehicles for exploring a universe of uncharted ideas."

So dream—but follow up the dream with action and ideas. Let it spark your creativity, not deaden it. Here's an example of how a dream became constructive reality:

> A young Baltimore widow dreamed of the great good she might someday accomplish that would give meaning to her otherwise lonely life. She dreamed of a Schweitzer-like existence in which she might go to darkest Africa and serve; she dreamed of becoming a doctor or a nurse; she dreamed of social work and education—but her own education and training were insufficient for any of these things. One day, some years ago, as she waited in a train depot, she began a conversation with a dejected student at the nearby university who was about to drop out for lack of funds. To help defray his expenses, she offered him free room and board while he finished his education. Since that time, she has given free room and board to many dozens of students. Today she still receives mail from her grateful boarders who include professors, businessmen, scientists—some as far away as Hungary, Afghanistan and Ethiopia.

STOP FEELING SORRY FOR YOURSELF

Dreams of self-pity quickly stifle creativity. Crutches like NO-BODY CARES ABOUT ME are frequently used for drowning oneself and one's life in maudlin tears. People who dream about how sorry friends and relatives will feel when they finally pass away have little time for dreams of accomplishment. A dynamic person simply has no time for feeling sorry for himself. Here's an example:

> An ex-convict, William Clark, had frequent opportunities to use crutches such as WHAT'S THE USE?; EVERYONE'S GOT IT IN FOR ME; and I HAD MY CHANCE—IT'S TOO LATE NOW! Instead of day-dreaming, though, he began thinking of ways he might help his fellow ex-cons. A few years after his release, he began giving hard-hitting talks on going straight to prisoners up for parole. They were extremely effective. Of the 5,000 men he has worked with, over 4,500 are still out of jail. Clark used experience as a tool rather than a crippling crutch.

Self-pity, incidentally, is basic material for dozens of crutches. To feel sorry for yourself is the easiest thing in the world. It doesn't accomplish much; it rarely improves anything; it saps the creative energies of man and is a barricade to human relationships. It seems to offer a gratification of its own that not everybody is willing to give up.

ACCIDENTAL CREATIVITY

Fate, divine providence, the stars, or whatever we may happen to believe moves the universe, has a strange way of inspiring the best in man from time to time, with the result that even those people who aren't striving to be creative often stumble onto some productive ideas. It's important to be alert and awake so you can take advantage of these "accidents" when they happen. The person who relies on mental crutches will be very apt to have his eyes closed when opportunity arises—or if they do happen to be open, he may find himself too weak mentally to respond creatively. The following case histories indicate the role "luck" can often play:

The first day of school began on a bright note for a teacher who was glancing over the rollbook. "Look at those IQ's," she thought to herself. After each student's name was a number, such as 138, 140, 145. "I've got a terrific class—quite an improvement over last year!" So the elated teacher tried new methods. The students responded exceptionally well to her dynamic approach. Only later did she learn that the figures after each pupil's name stood, not for IQ's, but for their locker numbers!

A co-worker of Duane Kelton, a junior executive, left the company to do free-lance writing. Later the writer accepted a job offer with a competitive firm and boasted to Duane of the $10,000 salary he was receiving. Some months later the competitor approached Duane and offered him a position, too. Before the interview, the young man began thinking of salary. "I have a more varied background than Dick. If he was worth $10,000 to the firm, I should be able to get $13,000." Since this was considerably more than he was making at the time, he felt he might need to prove his worth, so he spent several days preparing a unique portfolio which included an elaborate proposal of programs and ideas which he felt he could develop should he be accepted. He even included a dollars-and-cents breakdown of the return he felt he could bring the company through his ideas. He got the job—at the $13,000 he asked. Afterwards the personnel manager confided in him that the firm had been prepared to offer him only $10,000 but had been so impressed by his presentation that they gave him his asking price. It wasn't until some months later when his friend the writer was transferred into Duane's division that he learned Dick's $10,000 salary had been simply a boast to impress his friend —that he had actually been hired at $8,000! A "white lie" had stimulated Duane to prove his worth—and earn himself an extra $3,000 annually.

VAULT THOSE STONE WALLS

A dynamic person is fated to run into many stone walls in a lifetime—walls that have at one time or another been set up for a purpose but which are now a barrier to new ideas. These stone walls, combined with crutches like IT'S THE RULE; THAT'S THE LAW; or IT'S COMPANY POLICY can keep less dynamic brains inactive for years, or even for lifetimes. For the dynamic, creative person, however, such walls become a challenge, not a crutch. Take this incident in the legal world, for example:

Municipal court judge Lloyd Brown was concerned about the rising injury accident rate in his community and the fact that many of these injuries might easily have been prevented had the drivers and occupants of cars fastened their seatbelts. Educational advertising on the value of seatbelts seemed to have little effect on the public, so the judge confided to a fellow judge that he was considering increasing the fines of those persons involved in moving violations who had seatbelts but were not wearing them. The colleague warned the judge that he would be violating a law by doing this. Instead of stopping at this STONE WALL, the judge pondered the situation and decided that it would be well within his (and the defendant's) rights to *reduce by $5.00* the fines of those wearing seatbelts at the time of the arrest. This the judge did, and started a statewide trend which has been effective in promoting the use of seatbelts and reducing accident injuries.

STAY POSITIVE!

In summary, then, your dynamic personality must be a positive, enthusiastic personality, free from the mental crutches that circumvent accomplishment and self-improvement. Learn to recognize these crutches and their power—which might be best summed up in these parting words from our friendly "tour guide":

"The use of crutches can become a permanent part of anyone's way of life. This can lead to an ideal life—one in which change never rears its head, where ruts are deep and warm and comfortable, where people needn't ever trouble themselves with problems, solutions, ideas or other disturbing topics. In such a life, one day will always be like the day before it—and it will be free from surprises, excitement, anticipation, accomplishment, exploration and discovery. In such a life there will be no need to try new methods, new recipes, new colors, new fabrics, new words, new sound, new combinations, new games, or new ideas. It will be free from the confusing profusion of personalities that surround us today; there'll be no more smart people or stupid people, no humorous or serious people, no leaders or pacesetters. There'll be only people, each one essentially the same in personality and mental capacity as everyone else.

"We in the mental crutch industry have this as our goal—and we ask that you remember this every time YOU have the opportunity to use one of our products."

Keep it in mind the next time *you're* tempted to pick up a crutch!

100 MENTAL CRUTCHES—AND HOW TO BREAK THEM CREATIVELY

To rid yourself of mental crutches, you must be aware that you are using them. Start by listing a dozen of your "favorite" crutches. Jot them down on a slip of paper. Now list 13 of your own personal superstitions. ("Black cats are unlucky," etc.). Which of these can also double as crutches?

Next, list a dozen of your "fears." ("I'm afraid of high places," etc.) Check which of these also double as crutches. List a dozen of your fixed beliefs. ("Children should be spanked when necessary.") Any crutches here?

On another sheet of paper, copy these headings, then list the first dozen words that come to mind: I CAN'T; I REFUSE; I WOULDN'T DARE; I DON'T KNOW HOW TO.

See how many crutches a person can collect in just one short lifetime? How much more interesting can you make your lifetime if you rid yourself of some of them?

4

How to Make Time Work for You— Not Against You!

Take care of the minutes . . . the hours will take care of themselves.

Lord Chesterfield, 1749

1440 minutes! That's how many you have every 24 hours, to use as you see fit—1440!

It's also the number of minutes that are available to the President of the United States, the chairman of the board of your company, the author of the current best-selling book, a nation's top architect, the editor of the New York Times, the Mayor of Los Angeles —and the man in the next office who's slated for promotion.

Do you get as much done with your 1440 daily minutes as you can—or should? It all depends on you! What you accomplish in a day depends on what you *want* to accomplish in a day, because it's a simple truth that we make time for those things we *want* to make time for. Think about it for a moment. When you really want to play a game of golf—you do it! When you want to watch a World Series game or pro football championship or an Academy Award movie—you do it! You simply make the time available. Are you always that determined to make time for *other* important things? Are you getting as much from your 1440 minutes as you should be?

One of the "musts" in developing your dynamic personality is to learn how to use your time well and wisely. This you can do by *planning* your time, then defending that plan against a daily invasion of time killers.

CONSIDER YOUR TIME IMPORTANT

The first step in managing your time is to acquire a serious, sincere *respect for time*. Once you look upon time as a precious commodity, you will treat it as such and you'll be far more careful about wasting it. You'll find yourself as concerned about wasting time as you are with wasting water, gasoline, electricity, paper, postage stamps, food or money.

The second step is to *budget your time*, then stick with your budget. Put the important, much-desired things high on your priority list. Keep the time killers low on the list, eliminate them altogether, or turn them into something more constructive.

What are the time killers? Here's a partial list:

Television watching	Lunchtime
Phone conversations	Coffee breaks
Visitors	Small talk
Mistakes	Sleeping
Meetings	Correspondence

Each of these "killers" gobbles up your precious minutes at an unbelievably fast rate—at home as well as at work. The minutes they consume don't just add up; they multiply. Let's assume you spend a half-hour a day on the telephone; 30 minutes sorting through the mail, reading it, and writing your replies; 30 minutes a day on coffee breaks; 15 minutes talking with or entertaining visitors; an hour a day in meetings or other get-togethers; 40 minutes a day on small talk; 20 minutes or more correcting mistakes you've made. Already you have a minimum of over three hours "killed," even without the aid of television. Multiply this by seven days or 30 or 365 and you'll have some idea of what these time killers are costing you.

If you can't eliminate the time killers, try to handle them in a constructive manner. Obviously the "killers" include some necessities and it would be impossible to do without them completely, but it's possible to turn what might otherwise be wasted time into something stimulating or productive—or both!

TURN "WASTE TIME" INTO PRODUCTIVE TIME

Let's explore this, starting with perhaps the greatest escape mechanism of them all—*television*. If you're "average" you spend 3.3 hours a day in front of your set. Your children may well average 4.5 hours daily. Three or four hours a day! In a week this adds up to nearly 24 hours or one complete day spent watching the "boob tube." The experts say a child will spend 12,000 hours of his life in school—and 15,000 hours watching TV! What's the solution? Do you disconnect the set and say "No more TV!" Do you sell it to the highest bidder? Do you put a viewing limit on yourself and your family? Or do you establish some standards for creative TV watching and turn your viewing time into something to help you grow mentally? Here are some good suggestions from national TV critic Dick Sutcliffe, who warned his readers against watching for the sake of watching.

"Cut out wasting time on TV! Discipline yourself. Each time you watch TV ask yourself, 'Why TV now?' Is it a specific program you want to see? Good, watch it! Is time hanging heavy on your hands? Lift those heavy arms and turn the TV off. Nothing better to do? Then you're in trouble! Call a friend who isn't watching TV and plead with him to let you join him in whatever he's doing (within reason, of course).

"Make sure you use TV and that TV doesn't use you! Do you use TV to widen your horizons? Broaden your perspective? Deepen your insights? Or do you let TV use you to sell you products you don't need, recruit you for causes that really don't matter past next week, lull you with electronic pap that leaves you weaker in both muscle and mind at the end of the viewing time than when you started to watch? Select your TV fare with the same discrimination you would use in choosing from the menu of your favorite restaurant.

"Turn your mind ON as you watch. Pretend you're the director, producer, cameraman. How would you have pulled more out of the man or woman being interviewed? What would you say if you were there in the studio? . . . Use TV as a stimulant, not a sedative. Do you consider TV as 'home movies,' as a private and personal entertainment center in your home? Or do you consider TV to be a 'window to the world'? Select your programs on the basis of how they'll help you, not comfort you. Hesitate before you select the channel. Is this going to stir or lull me? At this moment in my life, do I need prodding rather than lulling? . . . Be willing to learn! If you have definite opinions on a pet peeve or project, is someone with an opposite point of view going to expound, advocate, argue on TV tonight? Willing to listen to the other side? Is it possible that you'll get even better arguments for your opinions by listening? Or will you be able to take it if the Other Side scores on you? And will the experience make you a little more mellow? Watch—for your own sake!

"Do everything in your power to let TV people know about the shows you've enjoyed and appreciated! Right now, grab the phone directory and copy the numbers of each of the TV stations available on your set. Put the numbers on top of the set so that the next time you start enjoying a program that moves, disturbs you or prods you, you'll be able to go right to the phone and dial the station, ask for the 'program director' and tell him—spontaneously, while the emotion in you is still warm (or cool)—your response to his scheduling of the show.

"Don't write TV off your schedule! Some of it is a waste of time, some of it a questionable use of creative energy and management money, but much of it is full of ideas and insights and facts that will make all of us better people for having seen and digested them."

A group of dynamic adults near Boston put TV to still another creative use recently. They met twice a month as an adult discussion group to share ideas and opinions on topics of current religious, political, social or artistic interest.

The group set aside one night a month as TV night, selecting an evening when a provocative topic was scheduled or when a particularly controversial guest was to appear on one of the interview shows. After watching the program, they would exchange their thoughts on the questions raised and the answers given. Many of these sessions lasted until the wee hours of the morning. The participants shared a feeling of exhilaration as well as edification.

Budget your watching time. Establish a maximum amount you're willing to spend with the electronic intruder and use the hours you save for more exciting, constructive things. Make a list of things you should do—or want to do "someday"—and keep it next to your set. Before turning on the next program, review the list to see what might more productively replace the time you are about to spend. Your list might read something like this:

Write a letter.	Read a professional magazine.
Read a book.	Play a game with the family.
Repair something.	Plan your vacation.
Paint a picture.	Write a letter to the editor.
Take some photos.	Redecorate a room.
Take a walk.	Tell the kids a story.
Try a new recipe.	Play the piano.
Write an article or book.	Clean out your desk.
Take a walk—or jog.	Visit the library.

The temptation will be great to fall back on mental crutches like I'LL GET AROUND TO THAT LATER IN THE WEEK or I'M PRETTY TIRED TONIGHT—I OWE IT TO MYSELF TO RELAX. Don't do it! Give your dynamic personality an opportunity to emerge—and break those crutches!

Let's look, now, at another electronic time killer—the *telephone*. Originally conceived as one of mankind's greatest timesavers, the phone today is often a gigantic headache, especially for employers, husbands, and parents of teenagers. Perhaps typical of the great amount of time wasted by phone is this study, conducted by a national business methods organization, on the working-day phone habits of a single office in a large corporation:

At the time of the study, the office staff numbered 26 people— three men and 23 women. For one complete month, the manager's secretary was instructed to "eavesdrop" on all incoming and out- going calls just long enough to determine the nature of the call and to time their duration. Her log staggered everyone:

Type of call	No. of calls	Avg. time	Total time
Emergency calls (trouble at home)	3	4 min.	12 min.
Menu planning	86	6	516
Plan evening's entertainment	41	8	328

Type of call	No. of calls	Avg. time	Total time
Shopping by phone	13	4	52
Instructions to housekeeper, sitter	28	5	140
Apologies, fights, etc., with lover	26	12	312
Calls for social groups	33	5	165
Calls for lunch reservations	94	3	282
Calls home: "Anything in the mail?"	25	5	125
Calls to weather bureau	6	2	12
From home: "Bring home a . . ."	32	6	192

The total loss from work production was over 35.4 manhours in a 30-day period—or nearly the full week's production for one person! The company's reaction was drastic but effective. All phones except that of the manager were changed to "inside only" lines and a pay telephone installed in the hallway outside the department. Time spent on personal calls for the following month dropped to less than two man-hours.

Similar logs, if anyone dared keep them, for housewives and teenagers would doubtless show a frightening loss of precious time on gossip calls and matters which could be covered in face-to-face conversation a few hours later. Businessmen are plagued, too, by calls which start out all business but end up simply chewing the fat. There are creative solutions to such phone problems, however, as you can see from the following case histories:

Jane Tyler had a neighbor who habitually called her three and four times a day. Each conversation would last from 20 to 30 minutes, and one day the conversations totaled nearly four hours. Her frantic "I must go now" was ignored by the neighbor who kept right on talking. Jane discussed her problem with the family and came up with two useful ideas. First, because she sincerely liked the neighbor, she was willing to spend *some* time in conversation, so she set up some "telephone chores" next to the phone —clothes to fold, sewing, mending, knitting—things she could do while talking so the time spent wouldn't be completely wasted. Next she made a list of "off the phone" excuses based on projects she wanted to work on. Instead of "I must go now," she used more urgent reasons such as "I have a dress to sew which I must finish," "I'm re-arranging my furniture," etc. Being an honest woman, she selected projects which she actually intended to carry out, thus getting more done than ever before.

Dana Braunell, an executive, was plagued by extended business calls which diminished his day's accomplishments. Finally, he placed a three-minute eggtimer by his phone to time the conversations. If the conversation was still going strong (unproductively) after the three minutes, he would terminate it with a suitable excuse about some urgent matters on his desk. He estimated a saving of 30 minutes a day as a result of the eggtimer.

Similar to phone callers as time killers are *visitors*. Naturally it would be a pretty dull world without visitors, both social and business, and obviously salesmen are necessary to the orderly transaction of business, but both visitors and salesmen can consume inordinate amounts of time—which means you must use some creative methods to cut the visits to shorter, more productive periods. Many businessmen with secretaries have a ready-made method for handling this.

One busy executive has standing instructions to his secretary that when visitors or salesmen arrive, she is to remind him in 15 minutes of a meeting at which he is due. If he is anxious to terminate the converastion, he will use this "meeting" to do so. If he wishes to extend the discussion a bit longer, he will ask her to "call Mr. So-and-so and ask if he would mind postponing it for another 30 minutes. I'll be tied up till then." This allows him more time, yet still establishes a stopping point for the conversation.

Don't let crutches like I CAN'T BE RUDE, or HE'S A FRIEND—I CAN'T JUST GET RID OF HIM LIKE THAT cause you to prolong unproductive visits or conversations. Be polite and use common courtesy— but be brief. You'll be helping the other fellow as well as yourself; his time's valuable too—or should be!

AVOID MISTAKES

Mistakes rank high on the list of time killers. Mistakes might be likened to our everyday lives as forest fires to our national resources. Just as terrible loss in timber and wildlife can result from a single carelessly discarded cigarette, so unfortunate losses of time can result from the smallest mistake. There are three basic kinds of mistakes which can cost you time, energy, and the confidence of others:

Mistakes in judgment. The results of wrong decisions made through preconceived ideas, prejudice, fear, stubborness, haste, incomplete facts, or incorrect facts.

"Honest" mistakes. Those caused by the unforeseen: dropping, tripping, falling, slipping, physical problems, momentary lapses of memory, forgetfulness, and misinterpretation of instructions or other peoples' acts or words.

"Planned" mistakes. Those we perpetuate through anger, orneriness or outright rebellion (either conscious or subconscious).

All three often require much creative effort to prevent tragic wastes of time. "Planned" mistakes are probably the most easily handled—once you become aware of them. Planned mistakes are simply those little acts of "sabotage" which many people tend to commit at some time. If you learn to recognize them as such, you can control or prevent them by determining why they occur, then taking steps to correct the situation. Here's an example:

An office manager noticed that the ditto reports typed by one of the girls in his section were carelessly done and loaded with typing errors and mistakes in spelling. The girl was a good typist, so he asked for an explanation. The only reason she could give was that her mind tended to wander when she was working on such routine material. This comment told the manager that she simply didn't consider the reports sufficiently important to be worthy of her best efforts. He solved the problem quickly and creatively. With the next assignment, he gave the girl a list of the persons to whom the copies were to be routed. It began with the president of the corporation and a half-dozen vice presidents. He was pleased with the immediate improvement in the quality of her typing, and he was convinced that he had analyzed the situation correctly when he overheard the girl tell a co-worker she couldn't stop for coffee break because she had a "report for the president" to finish.

Many "honest" mistakes happen this way, also. We often become careless when we perform the routine or menial task which doesn't require our full attention or interest. When we forget, drop, trip or stumble, we are in effect saying, "This was so unimportant that I simply didn't bother to think about it." There are solutions—many of them:

1. Treat even the most menial job as a creative challenge. How about a new format for this report? What's a faster way to do the dishes? Is there a more efficient way to empty the trash? What else might I pick up at the store to make the routine trip worthwhile?
2. Play games with the routine. List the unpleasant tasks; assign them a priority; change the priority; delegate what you can; combine as many as you can.
3. Stay alert! Avoid ruts. Keep your mind active and the rest of you will stay active. Mistakes seldom happen to alert people.

Mistakes in judgment are often the most difficult to avoid. Unfortunately they may have the most costly consequences. Snap decisions by the boss or others with authority to commit money to a project can influence dozens, even hundreds of others. The boss (or committee chairman or coach or politician) who doesn't investigate all possibilities and avenues of approach to any problem is leaving himself open to greater problems later on. Here's an example:

> In a moment of over-reaction to an emergency, the supervising engineer of an electronics company took two of his top engineers off their current project and gave them the task of solving an intricate controls process problem. They worked hard on the problem for a month and came up with 27 possible solutions. After the crisis had passed, the supervising engineer gave in to a suggestion that he allow a group of junior engineers to hold a brainstorm session on the same problem. Eleven men with scant knowledge of the intricacies of the problem met and attacked it in a non-critical atmosphere with no one commenting on any idea submitted. In 25 minutes, the "amateurs" came up with every idea the assigned engineers had generated—plus several extra ones.

Try creative approaches to help reduce the mistakes in judgment in your office, store, home, school, social group, church or political organization. Make a list, add to it as necessary, and keep it for reference when "decision time" arrives. Use this list for a starter:

1. Keep your mind open; be ready to try the unusual.
2. Get all the facts before you act.

3. Don't over-react. Haste can make more waste than indecision.
4. Admit you may not have all the answers. Ask someone for advice.
5. Be willing to brainstorm.
6. Let the past be a guide, but not your only one.
7. Profit by your mistakes.

Don't be afraid to make mistakes, but be ready to turn your mistakes into useful experiences by profiting from them. Remember, a "pro" is someone who doesn't make the same mistake twice.

DO SOMETHING ABOUT MEETINGS!

Meetings can consume hours of your time. Don't let them! Start cutting down on the number you attend. Attend only those which are relevant to your job or interests. Excuse yourself from the irrelevant and send delegates to those at which you aren't absolutely needed. If you call the meeting, make sure it's necessary; then see that it starts and ends on time; make sure it's chaired properly and that the discussion stays on the topic at hand; keep the meeting moving and don't allow it to be dominated by orators, digressors and diversionaries.

When you attend a meeting that drags on and on, walk out! Be your own time warden. Don't worry about appearing rude. If those who prolong the meeting are rude enough to waste your time, they shouldn't object to your refusing to waste any more. If more tact is in order, use the "another meeting" method. Have someone come in and wave you out, or have yourself paged or phoned after a specific time has elapsed. If it's not a business meeting, glance at your watch, look shocked and surprised, jump up and mumble something about being late for another engagement. If you're in a meeting where there's a lot of talk, but nothing of importance is being said, liven it up! Interrupt—ask questions, make provocative statements, take it upon yourself to suggest changes in the agenda or program. If you're bored, others must be, too, and they'll be grateful for your action.

Here's an instance where doing this very thing had positive results:

A dynamic young psychologist, just out of graduate school, joined a local psychological society. He found the members interesting but the meetings dull and the society's contribution to the community zero. So he made a suggestion: that the society have a speaker's bureau, through which they could spread the story of the function of psychologists to the whole community—an educational as well as a public relations program. Many members immediately volunteered and the next six months of meetings were devoted to setting up the bureau. At the annual convention, the young man was nominated for president of the society. He won.

Don't simply accept meetings as a necessary business or social evil. When that happens, you're leaning on mental crutches like WE'VE ALWAYS HAD 'EM—GUESS WE ALWAYS WILL and WHY MAKE WAVES? IT'S NOT REALLY SO BAD. Start your campaign now to make the meetings you attend more useful and meaningful! If all else fails, have luncheon or dinner meetings. At least you'll have only wasted your lunch hour—which is often lost time anyhow.

MAKE LUNCH A PRODUCTIVE TIME

There's no reason people should turn off their minds simply because they're feeding their mouths. The old rule of no business talk during lunchtime is a terrible time waster. You spend anywhere from four to five hours or more a week eating lunch. Why not put at least part of that time to some creative use? Here are three case histories which show the range of accomplishments possible during this "dead" time:

Beryl Tomlinson, the youthful president of a multi-million dollar Philadelphia publishing firm, has established daily luncheons, complete with wine, in his executive dining room. He invites 12 to 15 people, including suppliers, customers, members of management and members of the company's rank and file. The latter group may include truck drivers, secretaries, typists, artists, press operators, night shift supervisors, etc. In the course of a year, nearly all of the company's 250 employees have "Lunch with Beryl." Each guest is introduced and urged to tell something about himself and his job. The president then talks about company goals and recent achievements, complimenting persons and departments responsible for achievements. The result is a camaraderie seldom achieved in big business, plus one of the lowest employee turnover rates in the Philadelphia area.

A dozen employees of one large firm meet two lunchtimes weekly for a course in creative writing conducted by a former teacher. The results: some interesting discussions, plus published writing by six class members as a direct result of class assignments. Others who before were only "interested" in writing have overcome their lethargy and are now actively writing for the first time.

Three young supervisors, calling themselves "The Snoopers," circulate throughout the company cafeteria during lunchtime, sitting at different tables each noon, eating and talking shop with employees from different departments. They ask questions, learn all they can about the organization and operation of other phases of the company. Once weekly they lunch with each other to share the knowledge they've gained during other days and discuss how ideas used elsewhere can be applied to their jobs. These men are turning themselves into management timber by the creative use of their lunchtime.

The same principle applies outside the business world. Make lunch a time for mending fences or keeping friendships in good repair. Why simply sit and stare at a cup of coffee for lunch? Invite a friend or neighbor over; try new places to eat when shopping at lunchtime; plan to make each meal a productive use of time spent. One family makes an interesting game of their restaurant meals:

Whenever they eat out, the family plays a "game" while waiting to be served. They imagine themselves owners of the restaurant, and brainstorm ways in which they (as owners) would improve the restaurant. They discuss the decor, food, uniforms of the help, service, advertising ideas, and so on. Sometimes they give the results of their brainstorms to the management and as a result have been treated to complimentary drinks and/or meals for their efforts.

BREAK WITH BREAKTIME TRADITIONS

Breaks and coffee klatches can be used productively, too. Take them, by all means, but use them to expand your mind, not deaden it. Plan something restful but interesting. Play games, tell jokes, plan activities, discuss ideas, exercise, pursue a hobby, write. If that sounds like a lot in ten or 15 minutes, consider this. Most people take morning and afternoon breaks. That's 20 minutes or more a day, or 100 minutes a week. It's amazing how much you can accomplish in an hour and a half a week. In one office the girls play Password and other word games. They have fun and they've enriched their vocabulary as a result. A group of men in another office play ten minutes' worth of bridge at breaktime. One executive uses the time to write poetry and now has a collection of over 100 poems which he intends to publish one day. In short, any time you can carve out of a day should be worth considerably more than a discussion of office gossip, golf scores, dirty diapers, or your aches and pains. Keep your mind active all the time and it will automatically shun time-killers.

If you find you haven't anything to say during break sessions, put the old brain to work making lists of things to say, discuss, or do. Here's how one shy engineer solved the "silence gap":

> Donald Harris was highly competent on the job, but painfully shy and unable to converse with co-workers or acquaintances. He refused, however, to accept the mental crutch THAT'S JUST THE WAY I AM—I CAN'T CHANGE. To overcome his problem he made a list of ten subjects that would be of particular interest to his co-workers. He also made a "file" on each individual, noting items of common interest he might have with each. He used the lists to lead breaktime and lunchtable conversations away from the humdrum and toward stimulating topics. He succeeded in livening up breaks, increasing his circle of friends, and ultimately losing his shyness.

TALK ABOUT SOMETHING WORTHWHILE

This leads us to the danger of wasted hours through *"small talk"* —those inane conversations on unimportant topics like the weather, the price of pickles, or a town you visited back in 1955. Small talk costs you a fortune in wasted hours every year.

A memo issued to the sales force by a southern furniture company shows dramatically just what small talk can cost in dollars and cents. It reads:

Over 230 years ago, Thomas Fuller said, "Change of weather is the discourse of fools." As we put our "amen" to that, we'd like to add that discussing the weather is *expensive,* too! Want proof? Look: You make eight calls in an average day. Suppose you spend only one minute of each call (a conservative estimate) commenting on the weather. That's eight minutes a day. Projected over a year this is 2400 minutes or 40 hours—or a full workweek of conversation spent on how hot or cold or windy or wet it is. Starting tomorrow, rule out the weather as part of your patter. Instead of "Lovely weather we're having," tell your customers "Lovely furniture I'm selling." Instead of "It's hotter than #!##&% outside," say "Wait till you see my new samples— they're hotter than the weather!" You'll find this additional advertising of your product will result in some good sales increases —and we don't think Old Jupiter Pluvius will mind a bit!

The men responded and so did the customers. Sales rose by an unprecedented eight percent the first month of the weather-free campaign.

Start today thinking of ways to put any time *you* spend in small talk to better use.

DON'T SLEEP YOUR LIFE AWAY

Let's talk about *sleep*—that necessary time killer. But just how necessary is it? Do you need the amount of sleep you're now getting? Could you get by with less? You may never find yourself matching the feat of Ben Franklin, that active old gentleman who slept only four hours a night and used the rest of his time inventing, discussing, planning and developing. But—do you need every single minute you now take?

Look what some people have done by simply cutting a few minutes from their sleep time:

An advertising executive gets up a half-hour ahead of his family each morning and reads his stacks of trade publications, thus keeping himself abreast of the latest trends in his field.

A popular poet does most of his writing during the hour following his family's bedtime. From a single hour a night, he produces much of the verse for his syndicated column.

A married student does most of his studying in the hour before his family awakens every morning.

One businessman states that his most creative period is between the hours of four and five in the morning. He wakes up at four, outlines the day's activities, solves problems, and writes letters, then goes back to bed at five and sleeps till 6:30.

If you can't get up an hour earlier, try five or ten minutes. That won't hurt you and it can be good, productive time. After you've become used to ten minutes, try 15, then 20. If you can pick up even ten minutes a day you're 60 hours ahead in a year's time. Couldn't you accomplish a lot in that kind of time?

Saving time isn't the only approach, though. You can also make your subconscious work for you during your sleep and save yourself hours of time the next day. You simply "set the trap" before you retire. If you have a problem you can't seem to solve, think about it just before you go to bed. Review every facet of the problem, weigh and reweigh the possible solutions, then let your subconscious go to work on it while you sleep. You'll find many times that you'll be able to solve it upon arising in the morning. There's a secret to it, though. It must be the *last* thing you think about before dropping off to sleep. Don't think about your problem from 8 to 10:30 p.m., then watch the late-late TV show before retiring. Watch your program first, then set up the problem and go to bed.

TREAT TIME AS MORE VALUABLE THAN MONEY—OFTEN IT IS!

Thrift can become a time-killer for you. Don't let it! When Ben Franklin said "A penny saved is a penny earned . . ." he didn't mean you should spend a dime's worth of time to save that penny. The businessman who drives around town for 15 minutes trying to find a parking meter may save 40¢ under the parking lot fee, but he may cost himself several dollars in lost time. Set a monetary value to your time. If your income is $10,000 a year, your time is worth approximately 10¢ a minute; $15,000, 15¢; $20,000, 20¢ —and so on. Then use it as a guide to your common sense as to how to treat your time.

As a salesman for an international firm, Eric Stevens has occasion to travel in unfamiliar cities all over the world. He found a rented car to be his most economical mode of transportation in these cities, but also discovered that he wasted a great deal of time getting lost and asking directions. He determined he would solve the problem creatively by "asking for help" in a somewhat unusual way. Now, whenever he finds himself lost in a strange city, he hails a taxi, and pays the driver to drive to his destination, while he follows along in his own car. The taxi fare is more than offset by the saving in time and frustration for Eric.

RESPECT TIME—BUT DON'T WORSHIP IT

After such strong emphasis on the value of time, perhaps a word of warning is in order. You do not become a dynamic person by *worshipping* the minute. We're not suggesting that you race around day after day like the white rabbit in Alice's Wonderland trying to save time for who-knows-what. People who do this become creatures for which time-saving is an end in itself. Worship time—never!

Respect it—yes! Respect the value of a minute. Treat it with the same loving care you would give your stomach, for example, and fill it with something worthwhile, not junk. Give each minute of every day the same respect you would give to a dollar bill. Make time your best friend and constant companion, and you're bound to be a more dynamic person.

100 IDEAS FOR MAKING TIME WORK FOR YOU

First, give yourself some good reasons for wanting to save time. Take a sheet of paper and list a dozen projects you would like to accomplish if you "only had the time."

Below the projects, list 100 or more ideas for the creative use of your time. Let yourself go and just jot down the first things that come into your mind. Brainstorm; then select your best ideas and put them to use. List a dozen ways you can save time; list a dozen new things to do on coffee break; list a dozen new things you can do on Sunday; list a dozen ways you can make lunchtime more productive; and, finally, list a dozen ways you can make your next letter more interesting.

5

Learning to Use Your Mental Machinery

It is good to rub and polish your mind against the minds of others.

Michel De Montaigne, 1580

A man and his wife inherited a large but badly rundown house in the rural South. They decided to remodel it, but since their finances were limited they determined they would do the job themselves. They tackled the task with what equipment they had available—a handsaw and two hammers. The reconstruction took over two years of long hours and hard work, and the results could be termed, at best, "rustic."

Shortly afterwards, they discovered an old key that fit the lock on a door out back which they had assumed covered an abandoned well. The key unlocked a combination storm-cellar and tool shed which contained tools of every possible description and usage! There were power saws, lathes, and drills which would have saved the couple countless hours in their remodeling effort —and which would have enabled them to achieve a considerably more professional job!

You wouldn't attempt to build or remodel a home or a boat, or start any other major project without the proper tools at hand, would you? Of course not; yet this is something that happens to millions of us millions of times every day when we try to solve problems without using all of the mental machinery available to us.

And what an impressive array is available! Not only have you been blessed with the finest, most sophisticated piece of machinery ever devised—your mind; you've also been equipped with many finely developed creative tools, all in perfect working order and all ready for use at an instant's notice. When you try to think without them, you're being very much like the couple remodeling their house with a few primitive implements because they didn't know they had power equipment.

To be a dynamic person, you must be fully familiar with the tools of your trade; you must use them often, and keep them in good repair. What are they? Let's unlock your mental toolshed and take an inventory of the machinery available to you for building ideas. Every single one of these devices is yours, and even though some may be a bit rusty from disuse, you can and should start using them immediately for creative problem-solving and dynamic living.

Now, run down your inventory list:

Creative power tools

1. The enormous ENLARGER
2. The compact REDUCER
3. The mighty MODIFIER
4. The removable REARRANGER
5. The synthetic SUBSTITUTER
6. The sudden REVERSALIZER
7. The perfect COMBINER
8. The all-purpose ADAPTER
9. The idea RESURRECTOR
10. The systematic SEARCHER

Dynamic power source (the IDEA GENERATORS)

1. Self-propulsion
2. Partner-propulsion
3. Group-propulsion

Dynamic calculators (the IDEA SYNTHESIZERS)

1. The INCUBATOR
2. The EXPRESSION mechanism

The IDEA ANALYZER

The IDEA SELECTOR

Once you've learned to "program" your mind (Chapter 1), to recognize and analyze a problem (Chapter 2), to discard your mental crutches (Chapter 3), and to use your time effectively (Chapter 4), you're ready to get down to the nuts and bolts of being a dynamic, creative person and to actually come up with new ideas. This is where your creative power tools come into play.

These are the tools which will help you put your reservoir of experiences and knowledge to work. They are devices for associating two or more experiences in order to come up with ideas. The more frequently you use them, the greater you'll find your ability to generate ideas.

CREATIVE POWER TOOLS

1. The enormous ENLARGER. This helps you "think big." Many a good idea has come about by simply making something larger than it was previously. Try this device on the problem at hand. You can activate it with key questions like these:

> Should it be higher—wider—heavier? Can I make it bigger? Can its capacity be enlarged? How can it hold more? How about a bigger recipe? Should it take more room? A larger package? Why not sell it for more? Try it on a larger scale? Increase the volume? Make more of them? Use more pages? A bigger brush— a larger canvas? Make it louder? Longer? Should it include more people? More cities? More countries? Other planets?

The ENLARGER has been used successfully by nearly every industry with the result that we see "king size" in everything these days, from soap to cigarettes, from autos to airlines, from shopping centers to skyscrapers. We even see it in greeting cards:

> The sales manager of a small, struggling card publisher told his president, "If we don't come up with something new and different in our product soon, we're going to lose many major accounts to larger competitors." The president called his creative people together for a group "think session." During the meeting, an artist asked what were the best-selling cards of their competitors. "Jumbo $1.00 humorous cards," was the reply. "Then why don't we make larger ones—like $2.00 cards?" the artist suggested. "Don't stop there," said the editor, "Let's go a lot bigger and

make a giant $5.00 card!" The president agreed and the company soon marketed a greeting card measuring three feet by four feet which required a giant cardboard mailer and over a dollar in postage. Early doubts about public acceptance of so costly a card were dispelled when it became a whopping success with the youth market—the kids who'll do and pay just about anything to be different. Now the firm is working on a $10.00 card!

Obviously there are problems which you *can't* solve by an enlarger. You wouldn't apply that technique to solving the national debt, for example, or a flu epidemic. So turn to your next power tool.

2. The compact REDUCER. If "think big" isn't applicable, take the opposite approach and "think small." It's useful in solving more than just weight problems. Questions like these are the key to this little creative power tool:

Why not make it smaller? Try it in miniature? Simplify it? How about just half this size? Do you need this much space? Make it lighter? Shorter? Try to cover less area? Can you eliminate some of it—most of it—all of it? Use fewer words? Less art? Fewer colors? Can it be softer? How about making fewer of them? Taking less time? Spending less money? How can you use fewer people? De-escalate?

The evidence of the effectiveness of this "think small" method has been around us for years in compact and sports cars, mini-bikes, mini-skirts, bikinis, miniature radios, portable TV sets—the list is endless. Using a REDUCER needn't be limited to the automotive, electronics, or fashion world. It can work on problems of all kinds. Look how it helped solve this one:

After introducing flavored aspirin for children, a large pharmaceutical house became alarmed at reports that many children were swallowing the entire contents of the bottles—a potentially fatal dose—because they liked the flavor. The firm pondered the problem. Discarding suggestions for super safety locks on the lids, eliminating the flavoring, or using more frightening labels, it took a simpler course of action—reducing the number of tablets in each bottle. Instead of the usual 50 and 100 pills, the new bottles held 36, and instead of the regular five grains, each pill contained only 1¼ grains. If a child did swallow the contents, he wouldn't receive a harmful dose.

Simple? Of course, but someone had to think of it! Life, as we all know, isn't made up of simple "make it larger" or "make it smaller" solutions. You'll frequently find more complicated approaches are necessary. So let's look over the other tools available to you.

3. The mighty MODIFIER. If you can't live with something the way it is, don't destroy or abandon it—change it! Make it different. Nothing has achieved such a state of perfection that some modifications here and there wouldn't improve it. Such improvements might range from minor repairs to a major overhaul, from a little touch-up to a complete paint job. It often means a lot more work—but the results may well be worth the effort.

The ignition keys to your mighty MODIFIER are questions like these:

> How can it be revised? What happens if it's softer—harder—more pliable—more rigid? How about a different color? What gimmicks would improve it? How can it be given more value? Should it be temporary instead of permanent? What if it had a shorter life—or a longer one? How about a different floorplan —or format? What if you tried a different sound—or shape? Made it more humorous—more serious? What would happen if you changed the shape? Would it work better with wheels—or wings—or legs—or words? How about trying it in a different language? Revise the purpose or objective?

All around are hundreds of examples of modifications that have led to improved products, streamlined production or substantial cost savings, ranging from the U.S. Post Office which saved over $400,000 a year in maintenance costs by accepting a suggestion that they paint their mailboxes a solid blue instead of the usual red and blue, to this incident with far-reaching effects:

> The state of Ohio had a serious problem with strip mining, a system of mining which skimmed the coal from the earth's surface and left the countryside with gaping, desolate holes of dead earth. The public demanded an end to strip mining, but in a rare burst of creative lawmaking, the state legislators passed a more

constructive set of laws which required leveling the banks of waste dirt. The result changed disaster into asset for all concerned. Coal operators are now reclaiming the areas and finding that it pays. Trees, crops and cattle now thrive on the reshaped earth. One company converted eroded banks into game preserves and recreation areas. Another planted its newly contoured lands with trees which are over 25 feet high. A beautiful park was built on some 1,000 stripped acres donated to the state. It included fairgrounds, race track, ski slopes, lake and beach, an airport and picnic space for ten thousand people. Now, thanks to these creative "modification" efforts, business and land values continue to boom.

4. The removable REARRANGER. Elaborate change isn't always necessary. In fact, you may find yourself trying too hard to change something when a simple rearrangement would do the trick. Look at your problem from all angles to see if you have all the components you need to solve it. If you do, maybe you're ready to work with some rearrangements. Try it with these key questions:

What would happen if: you turned it upside down? Laid it on its side? Stood it on edge? Put it together differently? How about displaying it another way? Moving it somewhere else? Does it need another department—another compartment? What if you make the first last—or the last first? Why not move it? How would it work elsewhere? Who could do it better? What other machine might do the job more effectively? How could it be redistributed? How would it look on a different wall? In a different medium? How else can you divide it?

Any housewife can tell you that rearranging is an especially effective means of expressing yourself creatively, whether it's rearranging furniture, guest lists, activities, or meals. It can also be useful in solving "social" problems. Look:

Attendance at a woman's club had dropped steadily. Speakers became increasingly difficult to find. The new chairman was distraught and sought the advice of a friend—a featured speaker for the club a year earlier who had turned down a repeat invitation. "What's wrong with our group?" she asked. He pointed out candidly that during his last visit he had been required to sit through nearly an hour of committee reports, new and old business, and songs before delivering his talk. He had cut his speech short when he noticed members yawning and glancing at their watches. "The women were bored and exhausted by the time it was my turn, and it wasn't really much fun for any of us," he said. He suggested rearranging the program to place the speaker first on the agenda, followed by a question-answer period over refreshments. The business meeting would follow, "and your chairman of committees rather than the speaker would get to watch their friends squirm and peek at their watches—and would shorten their lengthy reports." The chairman made the re-arrangements, which resulted in increased interest and attendance —and her re-election to another term at the end of the year.

5. The synthetic SUBSTITUTER. Just as physicians today, once they've exhausted all other approaches, must decide to make a transplant of a heart or a kidney, so the dynamic mind must be willing and able to lift a problem from its present location and put it somewhere else, or to substitute something else in its place.

The substituter has been effective in many fields, especially in that of writing. Some unique pieces of fiction have developed using substitution: for example, Mark Twain substituted a peasant lad for a prince in *The Prince and the Pauper;* H. G. Wells substituted Martian invaders for a conventional army in *The War of the Worlds;* and in the more recently popular *Planets of the Apes,* the author substituted ape for man as the dominant creature in a future civilization.

Here's an interesting scientific use of substitution:

> One of science's latest discoveries is a radio transmitter that operates by "germ power." The electricity of this transmitter is generated by harmless bacteria feeding on sugar and living in test tubes containing sea-water. Scientists say this type of electrical power could eventually produce enough power to light entire cities and likewise convert solar energy to power uses and salt water to drinking water.

How do you start your synthetic SUBSTITUTER? With questions! Here are some keys you can begin with:

> What else would work here? A different sound—size—schedule? Serious instead of humorous—or vice versa? Honey for

vinegar? Soft sell for hard sell? A liquid for a solid? A conservative approach—or a liberal approach? A machine instead of labor? Hot for cold? The same idea in a new setting? A different power source? Facts instead of guesswork? A different time—or place— or person? Old for new? Leadership for pressure?

6. The sudden REVERSALIZER. Reverse your thinking! Travel the other direction for awhile and you'll run into many more idea combinations and possibilities. How often have you found yourself accepting an existing procedure or "truth" simply because "That's the way it's always been done"? Try reversing that procedure. You may find surprisingly good results.

An old Chinese custom was to pay the doctor a regular fee as long as the patient stayed well. Payments stopped whenever there was illness and until the patient's recovery was complete. Doing things backwards? Perhaps, but the practice fostered continuous attention to the patient's good health.

Ask these questions to start your REVERSALIZER:

What would happen if you put it in reverse? Try the unexpected? What if you face the opposite direction? Should you stop —or go? Transpose? Interchange? Retreat? Go slow instead of fast—or vice versa? Shut up instead of talk? Is this the time—or place—for reverse psychology?

And while we're talking about reverse psychology, look what it did for this midwestern grocer:

Weakening momentarily under a strong sales pitch, the merchant purchased more cartons of white salmon than he needed, even though pink salmon was far more popular with his customers. He tried unusual displays, price reductions, everything he knew, to move the white salmon, but the customers continued to favor pink. He concluded that the direct approach was getting him nowhere, so he tried a reverse approach. He built a small display of salmon and put up a sign that read WHITE SALMON—GUARANTEED NOT TO TURN PINK IN THE CAN. He quickly sold out of his supply of white salmon.

7. The right COMBINATION. While all ideas are combinations of other ideas or experiences, some are merely done subconsciously. Conscious combining can produce some interesting ideas. Try it. Ask yourself:

What would happen if you combined it with something else?
Can you merge them—marry them—or tie them together? Match
the unlikely? Combine opposites? Experiment with collections of
new words, new colors, new foods, new spices, new cloth? What
if you combined humor and tragedy? Combine the senses—taste
with sight, sound with touch, sight and scent? What if you combine the healthy and infirm, strong and weak, old and young?
Words and pictures? Legend and fact?

Our world today is filled with thousands of successful combinations, ranging from raisins with breakfast food, menthol with cigarettes and ammonia with detergents, to tigers in gas tanks and
fluoride with toothpaste. Here's a clever approach in which a Virginia policeman used a creative approach to combine reluctant
boys with eager young girls at a junior high dance:

> While chaperoning this particular dance, he noticed that the
> boys were typically reluctant to dance with the girls. The situa-
> tion improved somewhat, but there were still plenty of young
> misses for whom the evening threatened to be a dismal failure un-
> less action was taken. So he started conversations with the girls,
> and as a boy strolled by, the officer would take his arm and
> whisper, "What about dancing with my daughter?" Before the
> evening ended, this father of two boys had a dozen dancing
> "daughters"—and an invitation to attend the school prom.

8. The all-purpose ADAPTER. You can't possibly have all the
good ideas yourself, so borrow, beg or swipe them from other ideas
or other people. Look around you and see what's being done—and
what's been done in the past. Then use these key questions to turn
on your ADAPTER:

> What can you imitate? Adapt? Cross-pollinate? What success-
> ful approach from another field (or organization or philosophy)
> would work here? What recent inventions might help? How do
> other people handle it? What have the Joneses done? Where else
> can this idea be used? What is it similar to? Are there more where
> this came from? What else can I do with it?

Don't stop with a good idea until you've milked it for all it's
worth! If an idea is good one place, chances are it's good in another
—or many others! If the idea was yours, so much the better, but
if it's the other guy's and he's exhausted his approaches to it,

don't be afraid to use it as a starting point for your own ideas. That's how progress is made. Look how an enterprising "idea man" made extensive use of his ADAPTER mechanism to parlay a million-dollar idea into *four* million-dollar ideas:

> Stanley Arnold, who has built an entire business by providing major manufacturers with "million dollar ideas" to promote their products, had just concluded a highly successful campaign with a major seed grower. The campaign, timed to capture a mood of patriotic resurgence in the country, promoted the merits of "planting a flag" in gardens around the country, using the firm's packets of seeds to grow red, white and blue flowers. Before the promotion was ended, flags of flowers were blooming, not only in American gardens but in outposts all over the world—including the American Embassy in Moscow.
>
> Stanley then went to another client, a large tire firm, and sold them on the idea of using these same "flag" packets for a give-away promotion in their stores. The tire company had a successful promotion, and the seed company had a nice order for 18 million packages of seeds.
>
> A third client, a major oil firm, was impressed with the success of these promotions and asked Stanley to come up with a patriotic promotion for them. His approach was simple: the stations would give away an American flag decal free with every gasoline purchase. In a matter of months, millions of autos from coast to coast were proudly displaying their nation's flag.
>
> He then approached a fourth client, a national magazine, with the idea of promoting the flag via a decal insert in their January issue to coincide with the inauguration of the new president. They bought the idea and even went to press two weeks early in order to have the issues available to present to the outgoing president in the morning and to the new man in the afternoon of the only day of the year in which Americans have two presidents. One successful idea was adapted to three others—and four companies were delighted with the results.

9. The idea RESURRECTOR. Be willing to dig into the past for ideas and to resurrect discarded or unsuccessful ideas. A good idea never really dies, although you may find a rejected idea being treated as though it were dead forever. This is a terrible waste! Many an idea must simply await its time—and when that time has come, don't hesitate a minute to try it again. Here's a case in point:

In the late twenties a realtor called on several game publishers and tried in vain to sell a family game he had invented. Undaunted, he went "back to the drawing board" and revised it somewhat. It was the early thirties before he tried it again. One of the very companies which had rejected the idea initially, reconsidered and bought the game. The game seemed just made for the great depression and became an instant success and eventually a legend in the trade. In the nearly 40 years since that time, its popularity has literally swept the world, and the game has been translated into some 60 languages. As part of the game's equipment, its publisher prints more money than the United States Mint each year! The game? Monopoly.

10. The systematic SEARCHER. There should be no boundaries in your preliminary search for ideas. Nothing should be considered too far away, too high, too expensive, during the initial thought processing. If you don't find the idea you're looking for here, try over there. Keep looking, and use these questions to guide you in your search:

> Why not look elsewhere? What if you dug deeper—or reached higher? Who else can you ask? Where can you find more information? Should you ask again? Where else would it work? Why can't it be done here? What would happen if. . .?

For the dynamic person, the old expression "Let the mountain come to Mohammed" is not so far-fetched. In this shrinking world we live in, distance and difficulty no longer provide a formidable obstacle. Contemporary proof of this is a recent "happening" in Arizona:

> There was great skepticism and ridicule when a young Arizona draftsman suggested bringing the exciting sport of surfing to Tempe. "Are you nuts?" was the usual response, "The ocean's 350 miles away!" He didn't let this blunt his creativity. He set to work to develop a wave maker which could be used on a nearby lake. It took him a year to build a model in his backyard and another year to perfect it. Then he sold the idea to a large hair products company which uses surfing as a motif to promote hair coloring. They put up two million dollars for the project, and in less than two years, Tempe, Arizona, had a 20-acre "Big Surf" resort, complete with Polynesian palms and South-Pacific type

huts, sand beaches (trucked in from Phoenix), concessions, picnic areas, and surf!

These, then, are your ten basic "power tools" for use in developing your ideas. Perhaps you can accomplish some jobs with one; perhaps you'll use two or three. On particularly tough problems, you may find yourself needing all ten before you've hit on *the* idea.

Notice how each of these tools employs questions. These are your ignition keys. Creativity thrives on challenging the status quo, and these challenges usually have their beginnings with questions like "What would happen if. . . ?" or "Why don't we. . . ?" The questions we've used here are merely starters. Your questions should be geared to the problem at hand. One word of caution: avoid questions that can be easily answered by a simple *yes* or *no*. It's too easy and tempting to use that old idea-killer *no*. Make your questions the kind that take time and thought to answer. The purpose of these tools is to help you come up with as many ideas as possible in the shortest possible time, and once you learn to use them you'll be pleased at just how useful they can be.

YOUR DYNAMIC POWER SOURCE

Like any machinery, your creative tools can function only when the power is on. You must activate them. You must be able to turn on your creative power source when you need it—and as often as you need it. To do this, you should be aware of what power is available to you—and *how* you can turn it on. You must draw upon your creative generators, the IDEA GENERATORS. When you "plug in" your power tools, it must be into a source of energy. Something must start them to working. The kind of results you get will depend largely upon the kind of power you use, and the kind of power you use depends largely on the size of the project at hand. Let's take a look at three methods of generating power to activate your creative tools.

1. Self-propulsion. There will be times, like it or not, when you must generate ideas all by yourself—on the spot. In such instances, you must activate your mind with questions and ideas. It's something like a game of handball where you serve, catch and chase all by yourself. It's a good method for some projects. Many people prefer it for *all* their creative thinking. Others find themselves occasionally forced into such "solo" thinking, as in this incident:

> Walking down a city street one evening, a man was accosted by young thugs who demanded his money. He looked blankly at them. "Give us your money!" they repeated. He replied in sign language that he was deaf and dumb and didn't understand what they wanted. "Ah, the hell with it!" the thugs said finally, and left. He spent the rest of the evening telling his wife about the episode.

2. Partner propulsion. This time, instead of playing handball, you're playing tennis. You throw out ideas and questions and hit them around with someone else: a co-worker, supervisor, friend, parent, teacher, your mate—anyone with whom your mind can freewheel. It's important to select someone with whom you can communicate both intellectually and emotionally. But be careful— if you select an uncreative, unresponsive partner, you're back to playing handball again! Partner propulsion has been successful in the musical and literary fields, as evidenced by songwriters Rodgers and Hammerstein, and historians Ariel and Will Durant. It has also proven successful in advertising.

> A group of young creative people in a New York ad agency recently inaugurated what they call the "touch-touch, bang-bang school" of creativity. While they work, they casually hold hands or hug each other. Unorthodox, yes, but they point to many successful ads created this way. According to psychologists, touching can be an important catalyst at every step of the creative process.
>
> Conversely, emotional blocks prevent a person not only from fully using his capacities but also from going beyond them into previously unexplored areas, which is where a great many new ideas come from.

3. Group propulsion. If two heads are better than one for generating ideas, then why shouldn't four—or six—or more be even better? They can be, as long as everyone in the group is free to generate ideas on an equal basis. Group propulsion—or brainstorming as it's often called—can be tremendously effective in pooling the creative talent of many people to generate large quantities of ideas on any given topic.

The approach is simple, but it requires a few key ground rules. Here are some which will get your group-propulsion idea session off to a good, productive start:

1. Keep the group relatively small—between six and ten people, if possible.
2. No negative thinking of any kind! What you want at this stage is quantity. No idea is too crazy, too expensive, too impractical. Don't worry about whether it's been done before or didn't work. Judging the ideas comes later.
3. Define the problem or the area to be covered. Be sure everyone understands it.
4. Have a chairman who can prompt ideas when dead spaces occur, and who will silence negative thinkers. Keep the meeting moving. Ideas beget other ideas.
5. Encourage people to throw in an idea, but not to monopolize time by trying to "sell" it. Others will be waiting to present their ideas and may never do so if they have to wait too long.
6. Encourage piggybacking of ideas. Don't move away from one which is generating many other ideas until you're sure you've exhausted it.
7. Set a time limit before the meeting starts. If the well runs dry before time is up, adjourn. If the ideas are still flowing at quitting time, keep going as long as it's productive.
8. Encourage the use of *all* the creative tools.
9. Encourage group development of an idea during the brainstorm. Get everyone into the act and to feeling part of the finished idea.
10. Keep participants informed as to which ideas were finally chosen in the "judging" session.

Ideas will come thick and fast during a group session, and it's a good idea to have someone who isn't participating take notes. Every single idea should be written down, and the list kept even after "the" idea is finally chosen. The list can come in handy in future discussions of similar problems and may even save the necessity of later meetings.

Whichever source of ideas you use—self-propulsion, partner-propulsion, or group-propulsion—you'll get as much out of it as you put into it. If you approach idea-generation with a defeated, negative attitude, your yield of ideas will be poor. If you tackle it enthusiastically and full of confidence in the outcome, you can be sure of satisfactory results.

DYNAMIC CALCULATORS

Idea synthesizers are a must. Getting the ideas is only half the battle. You will usually have many dozens more than you can possibly use—this time around. Often, too, you will find they are still in the germ stage, or rough and unpolished. To complete your task of finding the right idea, you'll need two more items of mental machinery—the INCUBATOR and the EXPRESSION MECHANISM.

1. The INCUBATOR. Give your ideas time to take form and hatch properly. Don't rush them just for the sake of getting something on paper. Once you've generated your ideas, let them sit awhile. If you haven't much time, make the incubation period a short one—perhaps the duration of a coffee break or casual bull session—then go back to them. If you have more time, let them simmer overnight or for a day or two while your mind plays with combinations of the ideas you've already generated and perhaps comes up with a few new ones for good measure.

The best approach, as we've discussed earlier, is to sleep on it. Consider the problem and its possible solutions just before you go to bed and give your subsconscious a chance to mull it over.

2. The EXPRESSION MECHANISM. The best idea in all the world may never see daylight unless you can communicate it properly. Once you have connected all the elements that make up an idea, you must put it in written, spoken, or some other expressive form. Regardless of how you ultimately plan to communicate the idea, the first step is putting it down on paper, preferably in a single sentence or short paragraph.

If you find you can't express the idea so briefly, take another look at it. Either it isn't much of an idea, or you haven't thought it through yet. Be clear. Don't take for granted that the words you may use will always mean the same to others as they do to you. We'll discuss this vitally important phase of idea development—

selling your idea—in Chapter 9. For now, simply remember to express yourself well—and your ideas will sell!

THE IDEA ANALYZER

Now, your *creative tools*, powered by one or more *idea generators*, have given you a dozen, or perhaps even hundreds, of raw ideas. You've let them warm up and develop in your *incubator*, then you've *expressed* them in writing. Where do you go from here? How can one person, or even a group of persons, possibly wade through 500 suggestions and come up with the best one?

An impossible task? Not really. A housewife can walk into a supermarket which displays over 10,000 items, and in less than an hour come out with a week's supply of groceries. A man can walk into a large clothing store and in 15 minutes pick out a suit from a selection of over 500. There are more than 1000 different models, sizes, power combinations, prices, colors, interiors, etc., of cars, and yet we have little difficulty in selecting the one we want for a family car. Why, then, be overwhelmed by a list of 100 ideas regarding a given problem?

Your selection of the right idea will largely depend on your idea-analyzer mechanism. Let's see how to make this mechanism work:

1. Don't take a negative attitude toward any of the ideas at first. Weigh them all carefully.
2. Relate them to the problem at hand.
3. Toy with the ideas on your list. Try to combine two or more into a single idea. Prepare more information about each idea if necessary.
4. Now, group together the "impossible" ideas. Look at them again, very carefully. If you're still convinced they're impossible, set them aside.
5. Put the remaining ideas on separate 3x5 cards and sort and resort them by various methods.
6. Go through the cards quickly, picking the best and cutting the total number of ideas in half. Then narrow your selection down to the ten best.
7. Challenge each of your ten best with the appropriate *What? When? Where? Who? How?*

8. Show your ideas to the people who will ultimately be affected by them. Discuss each idea with the group and add any new ideas generated from your discussion.

If your analysis is thorough, you're ready for the "moment of truth"—the actual selection of *the* idea. For this, you'll need your final piece of mental machinery.

THE IDEA SELECTOR

If you were always to select the first idea that came to you, you wouldn't need any of the mental machinery we've discussed so far. But first ideas aren't always the best ideas, no matter how sound they may seem at the moment. For example:

The first approach to manned flight—equipping man with wings—was a fatal flop.
The first experiments with radium ended in agonizing death for many laboratory animals.
One of the first "cures" for a fever was bleeding the patient until the fever left.
The first solution to a crisis considered by many countries was war. Many such countries no longer exist.

Many, many times the tenth—or twentieth—or hundredth idea you come up with will be the one you'll use. Take your time and be selective. You'll prevent many future problems this way.

Once you've boiled your list down to the ten best ideas, your SELECTOR should help you pick your winner. Here's how it might work:

1. Judge the ideas on a time basis. Which can be used now and which later?
2. What will each idea cost? Which can you afford?
3. Which is the easiest and fastest to put into effect? Which should stay long-range?
4. Which will best solve the problem?
5. How do the experts react to the idea? Production men? The boss? Consultants?
6. Within the limits of time and material available to you, is this the best you can possibly do?

If time, budget and equipment permit, test your selection. Many times you'll find the expense of testing a drop in the bucket compared to running with the idea on a full scale. Continue to test and improve the idea even after you've put it to use.

Don't feel you *must* choose something from your final list of ideas. If the right idea isn't there, then back up and repeat the process over again. Few things are as costly as investing time, money and emotional effort in an idea that doesn't accomplish what it was intended to do.

NOW TAKE CARE OF IT

Quite an impressive array of machinery available to you, isn't it? Then keep it in good repair, ready for immediate use day or night. How? By using it often. Your creative tools will never wear out. In fact, they will improve with use. Your generator will never run down; it thrives on activity. Your calculators will actually become better and faster with constant activity. The only danger any of your mental machinery ever faces is *rust*—from disuse!

Finally, be persistent. Keep trying with your ideas. Each time they run into a stone wall, spring back into action with your mental machinery and remodel or replace the idea with an even better one.

6

Day-By-Day Development of Your Dynamic Personality

A man reveals his character even in the simplest thing he does.

Jean de la Bruyere 1688

When asked how he accounted for his team's stunning upset over the nation's number-one ranked college team, the football coach replied, "We were in better condition mentally. We simply wanted to win this one more than they wanted to win it. Physically they had a superb team and on paper they had every right to win by a healthy margin, but we had been thinking about this game all season. That extra conditioning made the difference."

Today is a very important day in your life! If you want it to, it may well be *the* most important—up to this point!

Why? Because today you go into training! Today you begin a training program which will result in a new personality for you—one which will make you far more productive and creative than you ever dreamed you could be. Creative thinking thrives on a dynamic personality—and a dynamic personality is a result of conditioning.

In the days ahead you're going to concentrate on conditioning those creative brain-muscles of yours, using many of your creative power tools from Chapter Five. You'll break old habits, form new ones, and in the process begin using your talents the way you *want* to use them!

In short, you're going to become a more effective, exciting person! Before you finish, you're going to find yourself doing your job better, communicating with people better, creating new, worthwhile ideas, and becoming more dynamic. Give it a try and watch it work!

This chapter consists of 30 one-day exercises—30 steps you can take toward developing your dynamic personality. Starting today (don't wait till tomorrow) take one step each day—and do it well. Begin using your creative power tools in every phase of your daily life. At the end of this chapter you'll find a 30-day training calendar. Use it as a diary. Record each day's creative efforts, then score yourself.

Before a week is over, you'll notice a marked improvement in your dynamic personality. By the time you've finished your "training period," you'll be ready to put all your creative powers to work for you.

Start by reading this chapter through completely, then follow each day's exercise one at a time. Ready? Let's go!

First Day

Be enthusiastic! Give your enthusiasm the ENORMOUS ENLARGER treatment. Be positive, cheerful, and optimistic about everything today: at home, on the job, in the classroom, on your current project—everywhere! Go through the whole day without negative thoughts, quarreling, or angry words. Enthusiasm is high octane fuel to your imagination—and negativism is its DDT! Approach everything you do today as an adventure, a challenge, a conquest, or an interesting event. Enjoy this day and fill it full of accomplishment. Heed the words of Thomas Drier who said:

> If we are ever to enjoy life, now is the time—not tomorrow, nor next year, nor in some future life after we have died. The best preparation for a better life next year is a full, complete, harmonious, joyous life this year. Our beliefs in a rich future life are of little importance unless we coin them into a rich, present life. Today should always be our most wonderful day!

Second Day

Be confident! Today's the day! Decide you're going to do it—then do it! Keep faith in yourself. Don't drain yourself with worry and don't bore those around you with your problems, doubts, and uncertainties. When problems arise just remind yourself that you are a creative problem solver, complete with all the tools you need to handle any task. Share your good ideas! Do whatever you're doing right now as if it were the most important task in the world, because right now it is!

> Konrad Adenaur once told a reporter, "A person can best get ahead by making himself important in the job at hand. Then he will not have to look for the next higher job—it will be offered to him. In all humility, I was much too busy being mayor of my beloved city of Cologne to waste time dreaming that some day my countrymen might ask me to be their chancellor. Yet that day came."

Third Day

Be curious! Use your SYSTEMATIC SEARCHER all day long. Ask questions today! Don't take anything at face value. Say "Why?" to everything, then respond with "What would happen if—?" when you're given an answer. Ask people about themselves, their ideas, their pet projects. They love to talk about them, and you'll learn something new. Talk with a stranger. Learn something new about your profession, occupation, or hobby. Discover something new about a friend, a loved one—or better yet, about yourself.

> Movie director Henry King urges people to "make it a point to stop and take time to make your own acquaintance. You'll probably get something of a surprise. Because you'll be meeting a very nice and stimulating person—yourself!"

Fourth Day

Be open-minded! Listen today! Listen to what the other fellow has to say. He might be giving you an idea, or the key to the solution to a problem, or some insight into yourself. If his point of view is completely opposite yours, listen even harder! Read a book with a viewpoint you don't share. Read it as though you were prepared to become a "true believer" of that philosophy. Then when you've finished, argue with it. Keep reminding yourself that there are many shades of gray between black and white.

For one full summer, Charles Garfield went to a church of a different denomination each Sunday morning. Some Sundays he visited two. His exploration took him from one extreme viewpoint to another, from the fundamentalist to the intellectual to the occult. By summer's end he had learned a great deal about his neighbors' beliefs—and in so doing had strengthened his own.

Fifth Day

Be a gambler! Stick your neck out; take a chance today! Try out that pet idea or program. Ask for that raise, talk back to the town bully, tell someone what's been on your mind for weeks. Give luck a chance to work for you. Take advantage of what Moss Hart called "that instinct or ability to sense and seize the right moment without wavering or playing safe." Without it, many gifted persons flicker brilliantly and briefly and then fade into oblivion in spite of their undoubted talents.

Character actor Kurt Brunner was to give a reading for a part he wanted badly. He was convinced that he had a better chance of being hired if only he looked the part, so he approached well-known makeup man Eddie Swift and asked if he would do the job —on credit. Eddie agreed to make him up on a double or nothing basis: Kurt would pay him double the usual rate of $50 if he got the role, nothing if he was turned down. The gamble paid off for both of them: Kurt got the part!

Sixth Day

Be concerned! Show genuine concern about others—their ideas, their problems, their happiness. Show compassion and empathy for everyone with whom you come into contact today. Don't allow yourself to become self-centered. Remember, a man wrapped up in himself makes a pretty small package. Help the other fellow solve his problem; you may have one like it yourself someday!

Gil Koch is a soft touch for panhandlers. He listens patiently to their pitch, then always gives them the dime or quarter they ask for. He admits this is partly out of compassion and partly because he is intrigued by the creative approaches used by many of these old fellows. One time, for instance, Gil and his attractive wife were approached by a derelict who asked for money, not for a cup of coffee but to buy beer. He gave the man the price of a beer. The old man thanked him profusely. Then as he was walking away, he turned and said with a toothless smile, "Say, Mister —I just wanted to tell you that I really admire your taste in women!" The couple agreed the incident "made" their evening.

Seventh Day

Be patient! Slow down and take it easy today. Give your ideas and projects time to develop and mature. Take enough time to give your creative machinery a chance to work for you. Don't let pessimism be a substitute for patience; give yourself time to achieve your goals. Cursing and kicking a stalled car or project simply wastes time and energy which could be used for listing more creative ideas for improving the situation. Peace of mind is too valuable to squander on small frustrations. A creative person has better things to do.

A woman remarked to the Polish pianist Paderewski, "You must have had a world of patience to learn to play as well as you do." "It's not that at all," he replied, "I have no more patience than anyone else. It's just that I *use* mine."

Eighth Day

Be emotional! Use a MIGHTY MODIFIER on your conservative behavior. Tell someone what you think of him today—or better yet, show him—in a creative way, of course! Your feelings play an important role in your creative makeup; don't hesitate to express them. Be a friend to as many people as possible. Remind your spouse of your love. Express your thanks for a gift or a kindness done to you. Share the tears of someone with a problem. (Then try to help him solve it creatively.) Remember, "Emotions are the color of life; we would be drab creatures indeed without them."

Don't keep praise to yourself. Someone else may need it more than you do. They tell about the old Vermont farmer who sat quietly rocking on his porch one spring night with his wife of some 50 years. Suddenly he turned and said to her, "Elsie, sometimes when I think of what you have meant to me all these years, it's all I can do to keep from telling you!"

Ninth Day

Be something better! Do something today for no other reason than that it's a good thing to do—for you or someone else. Mend a quarrel—share some treasure—keep a promise—forego a grudge —forgive an enemy—apologize if you were wrong—think first of someone else—be kind and gentle—sound off against malice— express your gratitude—welcome a stranger—re-examine your demands of others. Resist the temptation to become a gossipy old lady (of either sex) who thrives on tearing down other people. Albert Schweitzer said, "It is not enough merely to exist—you must do something more."

Daniel Thorpe, a 72-year old inventor, decided to "do something" after watching his blind neighbor struggle to keep his lawnmower in a straight line while cutting the grass. A short time later, he came up with a device which was a curious combination of a 6-volt battery, buzzers, a fish line, and adhesive tape. It straps around the blind man's waist, and, as he moves with the mower, one buzzer sounds if he's straying too far to the left, and another when he's too far to the right. The blind man can now cut his lawn in one hour. It used to take him five.

Tenth Day

Be a builder! Accomplish something—something you've put off too long already! Turn in a good performance today, no matter what it is you're doing. Deliver what you promise—but don't promise more than you can deliver. Don't waste valuable creative time and effort pretending to be something you aren't. Use it to make yourself more effective and productive. You can't build yourself up by tearing others down. Spend your effort creating, not destroying.

Wayman Creighton was criticizing the state and national penal systems at a forum on that subject, pointing out how little was being done to prepare convicts for rehabilitation to civilian life. "Then why don't you volunteer your time to help do something about it?" snapped the warden of a federal prison. The embarrassed speaker agreed to do what he could and, in cooperation with prison authorities, began conducting weekly public speaking courses for inmates who will soon be eligible for parole. His successful course is now in its tenth year at the prison.

Eleventh Day

Do something different! Give your SYNTHETIC SUBSTITUTE a workout today. Get out of that rut—and stay out! Shake up those brain cells by doing something that isn't part of your normal pattern, even if it's only opening a door with your left hand instead of your right, driving to work a different way, reading a book that's outside your field, or trying some new kind of entertainment. Anything is creative that requires some conscious thinking and planning instead of merely being performed by rote. These "little" creative acts can lead to bigger and perhaps more productive ones. Try it and see!

Toby Walker and his wife were confirmed movie and TV addicts—Friday night out to a movie, Saturday night home watching TV, Sunday night more TV. The resulting boredom was beginning to affect their marriage, so they decided to make each weekend "something different." Now their weekends include going to auctions, county fairs, art exhibits, church suppers, discothèques, sporting events, local festivals, motoring to towns they've never seen before, and so on. For this couple, each weekend is now an exciting "coming attraction."

Twelfth Day

Vary your routine! Examine those things you do daily in such a convenient set way and time. Why that particular way—or that particular time—or that particular route—or with that particular person? What would happen if: You got up ten minutes earlier? You smiled at breakfast? You read the women's pages instead of the sports page or vice versa? You got to work early—or late? You shopped in a store you've never been in before? You didn't watch your favorite show? You spoke up in the next meeting—or left it early—or changed its location? When you change a routine, replace it with a creative action or activity.

Arthur Hartley, a sales manager, decided to try a different type of meeting with his regional managers. So he invited the ten men and their wives for a four-day business-pleasure cruise on a rented yacht. During the daytime, the wives were turned loose on one of the nearby islands or port towns for shopping excursions, while the managers held uninterrupted meetings aboard the boat. Before picking up their wives for some evening entertainment, the men managed to get in some fishing as well. The cost? No more than the previous year's conference in a large downtown metropolitan hotel. The result? A very effective meeting—and some very happy wives.

Thirteenth Day

Learn something new! Today, program your mind with a new fact—a new skill—a new interest—a new insight into another person—a new song—a new prayer—a new aphorism—a new word —a new sight—a new point of view. Go to the library, visit a friend, enroll in a class, or simply ask a question. Take some positive action toward learning something new. It will come in handy creatively very soon.

Kay Goeller combats the routine that goes with the job of housewife and mother by taking craft courses. Each semester she enrolls in a different type of course and has thus far learned painting, sculpting, weaving, woodcarving, pottery making, copper enameling, stained glass designing, and furniture antiquing. As a result her home is beautified with many of her handiworks, she has enlarged her circle of acquaintances with creative people, she has earned extra money by selling some of her creations, and, perhaps most important of all, she has found the courses have enriched her sense of beauty and appreciation of other arts and crafts.

Fourteenth Day

Give a gift! Turn on that SUDDEN REVERSALIZER and turn off that selfish impulse. Make this a "giving" day. If it's birthday or holiday time, give a creative, unusual gift. Don't select something simply because it's convenient for you, pick something the recipient will like—something that will enrich his life creatively, too. If it's no special occasion, give a gift anyway. Thoreau said, "The best gift is a portion of oneself," so give of yourself today, whether it's an unexpected smile, a compliment, a helping hand—or an idea.

Douglas Uraneck gave his father a unique birthday present: he paid in advance for Dad to have a session with a fortune teller. It was a new experience for Dad, a writer, who subsequently became interested, not only in fortune telling, but also in those who go for readings, and is now gathering material for an article on the subject.

Fifteenth Day

Make a trade! Remember how, when you were little, you could open a whole new world by swapping a knife or marbles or a toy which had become commonplace for something exciting and mysterious—like someone else's knife or marbles or toy? It was a unique creative experience, one which unfortunately we tend to outgrow as adults. Revive it! Swap something today. Trade ideas, jokes, stories, or philosophies with someone else. Trade a good book or a magazine or a game you like to play, with another creative person. Expose your mind to their ideas—and theirs to yours.

Keith Watson, a young engineer, suggested a tie-swap during lunch hour one day for those who, like himself, had a dozen or so ties they didn't like and wouldn't wear. About 25 men entered the "big tie swap," and in less than an hour 500 ties changed hands. One of the men who came with only one tie, by some shrewd horsetrading left with over 100. Now the office girls are discussing the possibility of the same thing with sweaters, earrings, and other articles of jewelry.

Sixteenth Day

Do something with your spare time! What spare time? It's there—just take a few minutes today to review your schedule and see what is available. It may be time you normally devote to sleeping, eating, commuting, entertainment, or even working. Take 30 minutes or 20, or even ten, and do something creative with them. See how easy it will be to find the next 30—20—or ten tomorrow.

> Ted Jordan, a busy publishing executive, puts some of his spare time to use keeping in touch with his market—the public—via TV watching. He makes it a point to watch a different TV show each day regardless of how the show may conflict with his own personal tastes. He has watched prime evening drama, day-time serials, Saturday cartoons, Sunday religious shows, sporting events —everything. To preserve his sanity he limits his viewing to an hour a day, but he feels that by watching something different, he can better keep in touch with "what the other guy is thinking— and seeing."

Seventeenth Day

Do something just for the heck of it! Do something completely impractical today! Creative effort needn't always result in something productive or earth-shaking. Just the act of doing it may be fine therapy. It may help relieve tensions that are obstructing your creative ventures in other areas. Or it may simply be good for a laugh—and laughter is certainly good creative medicine!

> Malcom Capp, a computer programmer, observed that a computer-printer made different sounds as it printed, depending upon the number of characters in each line. If the line, for instance, had 40 letters, the printer would make a low note. If there were 100 letters, the sound was much higher. So the operator programmed a whole series of lines, calculated in advance to make certain sounds. The entire office smiled as they listened to his printer-machine play "Rock of Ages."

Eighteenth Day

Eat something different! Be creative when dining, too. When it comes to our eating habits, we frequently tend to be at our most conservative. From early childhood, we determine a list of foods we like—and a still longer list of those we don't like, or are not interested in trying. Times change. Recipes change. Foods themselves change, and if you retain your list of childhood taboos, you will miss out on some delightful and unusual taste experiences. Today, try something different—tea instead of coffee, a manhattan instead of a martini, lamb instead of roast beef, seafood instead of fowl, chocolate ants instead of peanuts. It can stimulate some new creative paths in the old brain—and you may enjoy your meal a whole lot more!

> Jay Tracy, a writer, decided to carry his creativity to the dining table, and when he and his wife went dining in a seacoast cafe he ordered whale steak—expecting the worst, but willing to "try anything once." He not only enjoyed the meal, but also ended up writing (and selling) a humorous article to a local magazine about his experiences. It was titled, "The Consumption of a Whale Steak as a Status Symbol."

Nineteenth Day

Wear something different! Dress creatively today! Psychologists tell us that the way we dress not only reflects our mood and personality—it also affects it. If you dress in drab, lackluster, conservative clothing, you can frequently find yourself becoming that way, too. When you choose lively styles and colors, you will find yourself becoming more alive in thought and action. Be creative in your attire! Dress as though you're going to a party, not a funeral!

> Jeannette Lee, art director for a major greeting card firm, confides that she pays more attention to the way an artist is dressed during an employment interview than she does to the artist's portfolio. "We've found," she says, "that a person's choice of color, style, and clothing combinations tells us more about his

sense of creativity than anything else. An imaginative dresser
is usually an imaginative artist—and vice versa."

Twentieth Day

Make a contribution! If you have the money, contribute to
some new charity or cause. If you have some time, contribute *that*
to your religious, social or professional organization. If both money
and time a little short right now, then contribute your ideas.
You'll find they are often considered far more valuable than the
tangible contributions.

Minerva Page, an invalid, decided not to let her immobility
confine her to a lifetime rut. She set herself a goal of writing a
letter to someone different each day. She began with close friends
and relatives, but, feeling she could do more, she got a list of
paraplegic patients from the local veteran's hospital and began
writing letters and notes of encouragement to them. Then from
the newspaper pages she made lists of recently bereaved widows
and wrote them letters of sympathy and encouragement plus suggestions as to how she (also a widow) had managed to find a
rich, full life. To some she was considered a crank. To many,
however, she was a source of inspiration and comfort during a
time of real need. Her list of correspondents is now in the hundreds—and her lonely hours are very few.

Twenty-first Day

Do your own thing! Put creativity first and popularity second
today. Do it because it's a good idea, because it's something you
want to do, and don't worry about what "they" are going to think
or say. One price a dynamic person often pays is being labeled
"odd," "eccentric," or "just plain nuts!" If this happens, wear the
label proudly because it means you're willing to try the new—to
be a dynamic person.

"A grown man playing with toys!" they said of Morry Stone,
a publisher whose hobby is collecting and making model streetcars, but he ignored them and continued to enjoy his unusual
hobby. He gathers pictures and drawings of old streetcars, de-

velops his own plans, then builds accurate scale models, complete with small motors and a set of tracks. He communicates with other collectors around the world, exchanging plans and ideas, and has built up a wide circle of interesting acquaintances. His collection is now valued at several thousand dollars.

Twenty-second Day

Say something different! Stay out of *verbal* ruts, too. Don't rely on stock questions or phrases to carry you through today. Conversations of the "Hello-and-how-are-you today-I'm-fine-thanks-and-yourself" variety are both unproductive and creatively unstimulating. Increase your vocabulary, even if it's only by one new word a day. Make your greetings meaningful, not just routine. Use your ALL-PURPOSE ADAPTOR, if necessary, and borrow some conversation techniques from the "experts." Make it a point today to say something that will shake both you and someone else out of a conversational rut.

> Franklin Roosevelt, irritated by the constant exchange of meaningless clichés during official Washington receptions, decided one evening to test whether or not people even listened to what was said during small talk. To each guest coming down the noisy reception line, he would flash the famous Roosevelt smile and say, "I murdered my grandmother last night," to which guests replied "Thank you—I'm happy to be here," or "Yes, it looks like an excellent crowd tonight." He had welcomed over a hundred people in this manner before one guest smiled and responded, "Well, she certainly had it coming!"

Twenty-third Day

Choose a new friend! You don't know all the interesting people you'd like to know—do you? Then make today the day you start a new friendship with someone interesting and creative, someone who can help you out of a rut. The way, of course, to have interesting friends is to be one yourself, so turn your talents toward making yourself interesting to your friends, old and new. Use your PERFECT COMBINER mechanism to come up with some new "people combinations." Invite someone different to lunch—or on a shopping trip, to church—or out for an evening's entertainment. Then talk to them—communicate with them. Bored people beget nothing but more bored people; small talk begets more small talk; but dynamic people stimulate other dynamic people—and this is how ideas are born!

Ronald Fiske balked at having to face another cocktail party and its boring small talk, so his wife threw him a challenge. "Why don't you do something about it instead of just avoiding parties?" So he began making a point of turning "cocktail party conversation" from the mundane to a stimulating discussion on topics of current interest—politics, drugs, morality, creativity. He lost a few "friends" this way, but made more new ones. He also became known as a more interesting person, a better-informed citizen, and has since become active in community affairs.

Twenty-fourth Day

Decide to communicate! Make it a point today to reach someone about an important subject—to really communicate! Know what you want to say. Think it out before you say it; be simple, forthright and constructive. Be prepared. Gather your thoughts in an orderly way and present them in the same manner. Remember, you may only have the floor for a short time, so be ready to make the best of it. Be brief. If it's a good idea, it can be sold quickly. If it's not, 1000 pages won't help. Remember, there are three basic ways we humans have to communicate with one another —conversation, writing, or action. Decide which of them will best suit your present situation. Or you may need to use all three, as did this enterprising wife:

Loretta Teller saw less and less of her psychiatrist husband as his practice grew and prospered. He would promise to "get around to our long overdue talk very soon"—but it didn't happen. She wrote notes and pinned them to his coat, but still he never quite "found the time." Finally, she called his receptionist and using an assumed name made an appointment with her husband. She arrived, locked the office door, plunked down her $30 fee, and demanded her hour of talking time. The astonished but amused psychiatrist set up standing daily appointments with his wife from then on—for free.

Twenty-fifth Day

Listen! Communication is a two-way radio. Until you've heard and understood what the other fellow is saying, you haven't really communicated with him. Use your REMOVABLE REARRANGER to help you listen instead of talk. Listening can be hard work, but it pays off. Listen to what the other guy has to tell; he may have some good ideas for you! Today, listen to everyone who talks to you. Hear him completely through before you plan your "rebuttal" or before you try to communicate your own ideas. Listen as though the information you are about to receive were the most important of your whole life. Who knows—it might well be!

> Irving Stone, one of the outstanding men in his field, is held in awe by many because of his remarkable grasp of what the public likes—and will buy. When asked about this apparent "instinct" for public taste, he replied, "There's no instinct to it— I'm simply a good listener. I go into stores where my products are sold and I listen. Listen to customers' comments when they're buying or not buying the product. I listen when the sales clerks tell me what's selling and what isn't. And I listen when store owners, managers, and buyers tell me what sells for them. Other manufacturers would rather talk about how good their product is. I've found that good listeners generally make more sales than good talkers."

Twenty-sixth Day

Write a creative letter—a friendly one! Write a letter that will interest and stimulate the party at the other end, whether he be a customer, client, relative, or friend. Use your letters to convey ideas and to collect others, not merely to say, "Having a fine time, wish you were here." Make the letter interesting; talk to the recipient as though you were right there in the room together. Use your sense of humor, don't make it a stuffy letter. Throw in some extra item of interest: a funny cartoon you've clipped, a newspaper or magazine article, some photos, a lock of hair, a swatch of material. Make the letter attractive: use decorative notepaper or stationery and keep it neat and legible. When you're writing, use narration, anecdotes, quote others, ask questions. Work at keeping it brief (your COMPACT REDUCER will help here) but meaty. It may take longer, but remember, a good letter is well worth whatever time you have had to spend on it.

Micki Spitz decided to pep up mail call for her overseas GI husband, so in addition to her daily letters, she began working on a long narrative of her daily experiences: run-ins with the boss, conversations with some of his old friends, etc., reviews of movies she had seen and books she had read. At the end of three months, she taped the letters end to end and shipped them in a package to her husband, who became the first GI to receive a letter nearly a half-mile long!

Twenty-seventh Day

Write a creative letter—an angry one! Sound off today on whatever has been bugging you! Whatever is disturbing you—from politics, morals, the state of the union, how the company's being run, to the educational system—let someone know about it. Write a letter to someone who is in a position to do something about it: your congressman, mayor, principal, corporation president, newspaper editor, or church body. But do your complaining in a constructive, creative manner. Let your feelings be known, but in a tactful, intelligent way; don't berate or browbeat the party at the other end. Offer a positive suggestion for improving the situation —don't just criticize. Remember the old saying, "It's better to light one candle than to curse the darkness!"

William Osgood, a parent of seven, was disturbed about the rising rate of smoking among young people, especially those of college age, so he wrote the governor of his state to express these feelings. Rather than dwell on the evils of tobacco or other negative points, he made these constructive suggestions:

1. That cigarette vending machines can and should be kept out of community colleges.
2. If the governor's office would send him the names and addresses of the members of the Board of Education, he would gladly write personal letters to them, asking them to wait until

summer, then remove the machines from the schools, and to pass rules keeping them out.

3. He realized these steps would not prevent students from smoking, but felt that removing the temptation might be a good starting point.

The vending machines were subsequently removed from the school's buildings.

Twenty-eighth Day

Let your actions speak louder than words! There's a time for talking and a time for action. Make today the time for action! Communicate your ideas by demonstrating them and how they work. If a picture is worth a thousand words, then a well-timed, well-conceived action like a pat on the back, a handshake, a hug or a kiss, is worth ten thousand—or more. Give a live demonstration, set an example, or show your sincerity by "putting your money where your mouth is." Show someone what you're thinking—today!

Ed Lake, president of a small corporation, determined that he and his 14 top men were collectively some 120 pounds over-weight, and as such were all likely cardiac candidates. Gentle jibes to his staff bore little or no results, so Ed decided to take more dramatic action. He founded the ICATLYC (I Can't Afford to Lose You Club). Each of his executives were automatic members, and as such were given their optimum weight by the company doctor and a time limit in which they were to shed the dangerous pounds. Each member who met the deadline received the equivalent of $1\frac{1}{2}\%$ of his annual salary, with the bonus to recur each year as long as the man kept his "healthy weight." A $20,000-a-year man, for example, could gain $300 a year just for keeping trim. In six weeks, ten of the 14 men had lost 80 collective pounds!

Twenty-ninth Day

Turn barriers into bridges! Overcome some obstacle today—and put it to work for you. What separates you from those with whom you want to communicate? Words—actions—background

—temper—attitude? Isolate your problem, then work at solving it creatively. Remember, to communicate we must transport ourselves and our ideas from our own private world into that of another. It requires ingenuity and effort, but the results are well worth it.

Clarence Jordan, a minister in the rural South, felt frustration at being unable to convey the Gospel message to many of the semi-illiterate tenant farmers around him. Whenever he read to them from the Bible, their faces registered puzzlement, then indifference. They simply couldn't grasp ideas presented in King James English. So he wrote a complete "Cotton Patch" translation of the Bible, putting the timeless stories into the language of the tenant farmer, using words and dialect which spoke to the uneducated, yet which were rich and vivid enough to add beauty and meaning to all readers. It worked. Not only was he able to reach his "flock" with the translations—his Cotton Patch translations have since been published in book form and on records for sale and distribution all across the nation.

Thirtieth Day

Try again! Get out the IDEA RESURRECTOR and put it to work. Today's the perfect day to try again with an idea that flopped yesterday, or last week, or last year! You're a day, or a week, or a year smarter now than you were before. Take the idea out of storage, dust it off, improve it and bring it up to date. Use your creative machinery to reshape the idea if necessary. Be sure that everyone who might be interested sees it. Circulate it. Try again!

A father noticed that his ten-year old son became easily discouraged when his projects didn't work out and would quickly give them up for good. One evening Dad handed the youngster a thin board and a penknife and asked him to scratch a line across the width of the board. The board and the knife were then locked in a desk. The ritual was performed each evening, and the boy would draw the knife along the deepening groove. The lad became increasingly curious—until one night there was no more groove. His last light movement of the knife had cut the board in two. The father said to his boy, "Did you realize this was possible with so little effort? Remember, son, success or failure in

Your Dynamic Personality Training Calendar . . .

INSTRUCTIONS:

Taking each new creative assignment one day at a time, put it into action.
Under HOW, jot down what you did for the assignment. (Ex.: *Vary your routine*—Took wife to dinner.)
Under RESULTS, post how successful you were. (Ex.: Made wife happy, learned how to eat lobster.)

SCORE YOUR-SELF

If you feel your handling of the assignment was very successful and you improved your creative powers, score yourself a *3*.
If you were fairly successful, give yourself a *2*.
If you tried, even though things didn't work out, take a *1*.
If you made no effort, rate yourself *0*.
After 30 days, total your score. If you had 30 3's, give yourself 10 bonus points. Now, see how you rate:
90–100 Excellent
79–89 Good work!
60–78 Creative
59 and below—
Try again!

1 *Be enthusiastic!* HOW: RESULTS: Score:	2 *Be confident!* HOW: RESULTS: Score:	3 *Be curious!* HOW: RESULTS: Score:
8 *Be emotional!* HOW: RESULTS: Score:	9 *Be something better!* HOW: RESULTS: Score:	10 *Be a builder!* HOW: RESULTS: Score:
15 *Made a trade!* HOW: RESULTS: Score:	16 *Do something with your spare time!* HOW: RESULTS: Score:	17 *Do something just for the heck of it!* HOW: RESULTS: Score:
22 *Say something different!* HOW: RESULTS: Score:	23 *Choose a new friend!* HOW: RESULTS: Score:	24 *Decide to communicate!* HOW: RESULTS: Score:
29 *Turn barriers into bridges!* HOW: RESULTS: Score:	30 *Try again!* HOW: RESULTS: Score:	

4 *Be open-minded!* HOW: RESULTS: Score:	5 *Be a gambler!* HOW: RESULTS: Score:	6 *Be concerned!* HOW: RESULTS: Score:	7 *Be patient!* HOW: RESULTS: Score:
11 *Do something different!* HOW: RESULTS: Score:	12 *Vary your routine!* HOW: RESULTS: Score:	13 *Learn something new!* HOW: RESULTS: Score:	14 *Give a gift!* HOW: RESULTS: Score:
18 *Eat something different!* HOW: RESULTS: Score:	19 *Wear something differ-ent!* HOW: RESULTS: Score:	20 *Make a contribution!* HOW: RESULTS: Score:	21 *Do your own thing!* HOW: RESULTS: Score:
25 *Listen!* HOW: RESULTS: Score:	26 *Write a crea-tive letter (friendly)* HOW: RESULTS: Score:	27 *Write a crea-tive letter (angry)* HOW: RESULTS: Score:	28 *Let actions speak louder than words* HOW: RESULTS: Score:

life doesn't always depend so much on how hard you try, but on whether you keep at it!"

Why is it so important to have a dynamic personality? Because once you have accomplished this, everything you do will be done creatively. You will *want* to tackle problems creatively—to handle your job creatively—to raise your family creatively—to think and act creatively—because it's all a part of your dynamic makeup. You will find that you're no longer satisfied with the rut that seemed so comfortable and secure. You're ready to nourish that urge to explore—expand—and create. You're ready to take the real "you" out of its hiding place and make it the productive, vital person you were intended to be!

Whether you finish this book in one evening, or a week, or a month, doesn't matter. Start now, using the calendar on the next pages, and keep your 30-day training period up-to-date. Come back to this chapter as often as necessary to refresh your memory, then make each day a step towards developing a strong, *permanent,* dynamic personality.

To use this calendar, copy the chart given on pages 112 and 113 onto a large piece of paper, big enough to allow room for writing in each block. For 30 consecutive days, record your success at accomplishing your "training assignment." Watch your creative ability increase as your dynamic personality develops.

7

How to Use Your Imagination to Increase Your Income

There are two reasons for trying anything—
to succeed and to make money.

Gilbert

Do you want to lead a more exciting life? Make more money!

It's a fact. A recent Gallup poll asked Americans, "Do you find life exciting, routine, or dull?" Not so strangely, people tended to classify their lives exciting or dull in almost direct relationship to their incomes. Of those with incomes of $15,000 and over, nearly 70% said they found life exciting, as did 62% of those in the $10-15,000 bracket. Only 49% of those in the $7-10,000 and 47% of those in the $5-$7,000 range, however, found life exciting. Of those in the under-$5,000 range, nearly 80% said life for them was routine or dull. Naturally, you didn't need a book to tell you that it's better to have money than not. But perhaps we *can* be useful by providing you with some good creative suggestions on HOW to turn your good ideas into money, which in turn can help you lead a more exciting, rewarding life.

Money, of course, isn't the only incentive for being creative—but it's a darned good one. Why not make your ideas pay? Thousands of people do just that every day of the year.

The experts tell us there are some six basic "needs" for which a man will part with his money willingly. If you want to determine the value of an idea, test it against these basics. If the idea hits one or more, there's a good chance you have something that somebody, somewhere, will be willing to buy. Look over the six "basics." Read them several times. Then keep them in mind as you come up with your ideas.

Under normal circumstances, a man will spend money for anything that will:

1. *Make him more money.* Increase his earnings and profits, earn dividends, help him save money, or otherwise augment his wealth.
2. *Serve his basic needs.* Keep him and his family healthy, safe from harm, and reasonably comfortable and secure.
3. *Build his image.* Insure his fame or help him to be well thought of by his fellow men.
4. *Give him pleasure.* Please his senses of taste, touch, smell, hearing or speech, provide him with psychological satisfaction, or stimulate his curiosity and spirit of adventure.
5. *Provide him with a worthwhile service.* Offer him something that will benefit himself and his family, his country, his company, or his loved ones—now or in the future.
6. *Enhance his personal power.* Enable him to increase his ability either mentally or physically, to be more effective in controlling himself or others—or both.

Naturally, certain of these basic needs will be more important to some people than to others, and different people will establish different priorities. One man may be very interested in making money and care very little about his "image." Another may be far more pleasure-oriented. The price of *anything* is determined by just how badly the buyer wants or needs what you're selling. For instance:

—A plain bar of iron is worth $5.
—This same piece of iron made into horseshoes would sell for $10.50.
—Make it into needles and it would be worth $3,000.
—If it were made into balance springs for watches, its total value would be around $250,000.

Too often, when you find the old paycheck simply won't stretch far enough to take care of the budget, you start working on a new budget—one that cuts back here, eliminates something there, and postpones a dream or two. Don't! Don't worry yourself into an ulcer or budget yourself into perpetual boredom! Take a positive approach. Use your creative powers to make more money —to increase your *income*, not your list of *"can'ts."* How?

If you have a job, take a more dynamic approach to it: earn yourself a raise, a bonus, an award, or perhaps even a piece of the action! (More about this in the next chapter.) If you're the inventive type—invent! But be sure you aim your efforts toward one or more of the six basic needs. If you're a retailer, be more dynamic in persuading the customer to buy *more* from you. If you're a manufacturer, come up with new products that appeal to the public's basic needs, or make creative improvements on your present products to make them more appealing. If you're someone with a normal 24-hour day, use your spare time, your creative ideas and your talents to earn money or additional income on a part-time basis.

What do you need to make money?

An idea—and time. Time to develop it, time to sell it, time to put it into action. If you have one of those so-called "24-hour-a-day" jobs, take a good, hard second look at it. Is it paying you what you want and need to live the way you want to live? If not, then don't let it consume 24 hours a day. Put it into its proper perspective. How much time should you set aside for *you* and what *you* want to do?

An idea—and talent. Talent enough to see your idea through to fruition, or talent enough to explain it well to someone with specialized talents; imagination that enables you to see something that nobody else sees. If there's something you can do and are good at doing, do it! Put some good creative thought into ways of doing it better, but at least do it! The words "I've always wanted to do that but I just never got around to it" are an admission of a terrible waste of time and talent.

An idea—and some treasure. It takes money to make money— sometimes. Sometimes *other* treasure will do, whether household items, friends, family, real estate, buildings, raw materials, art objects, machinery, or even space. Take inventory: you may find you have far more treasure than you realized. Whether you're highly creative, just average, or barely hanging on, you have a certain amount of all three of these salable commodities—time, talent, and treasure. It's *how* you use them that can mean money (or lack of it) to you. You must learn to effectively combine your imagination with the six basic needs.

Let's spend this chapter looking over a variety of ways other dynamic people have aimed their time, talents or treasure toward those basic needs to come up with good, salable ideas—and make themselves some money in the process.

IDEAS THAT MAKE MONEY

If you have ideas that will help a man to increase his personal wealth, or a company to enlarge its profit picture, they are valuable. Most business firms are very aware that good ideas can save them money, thus increasing their profits, or make more money for them, thus increasing their volume. In either case, they consider it good business to encourage ideas by offering awards and bonuses for them. If your employer has a paid suggestion program, contribute your ideas to it. If he doesn't, suggest that he start one.

> Fred Simpson, an employee of a major automobile manufacturer, has been making his ideas pay off for over 20 years. Taking advantage of his company's employee suggestion plan, Fred has submitted over 500 suggestions during his period of employment —and has had over 100 of these accepted. Three times he has won the company's maximum payoff award for amounts of $10,000, $6,000 and $5,000. He made his first suggestion while still an apprentice, received a $25.00 award, and has been at it ever since. Fred says the key to his success has been simply to keep his eyes open and not be afraid to submit an idea. He notes that many people turn in one idea and get it rejected, so they climb onto their mental crutches and stop trying. Fred didn't, to the delight of his company—and his family.

If you can put your talents to use serving the basic needs of an individual, a corporation or a state, you'll usually find a ready market for them. If you can do something, and do it well, you can always find somebody somewhere who will be willing to pay you for your services.

EXPERIENCE, INC. was the name chosen by a group of retired men who felt they still had valuable services to render, even though they were "over 65." The men—accountants, executives, sales managers, production people, purchasers, etc.—offer their services on a part-time or consulting basis to smaller businesses or newer firms who cannot yet afford full-time persons with their kind of experience. The firms who "rent" them are delighted with the help they provide, as well as with the training they are able to give the less-experienced employees, and the men themselves are pleased to have the opportunity to be useful as well as to supplement their retirement income.

And who says that "servicing basic needs" should always be limited to people? Pets, for example, have problems too, and they (and their masters) are grateful for creative ideas for solving them.

One enterprising dog owner was concerned about his cocker spaniel's problem of its long ears flopping in and around its food as it ate. So he devised an "ear guard" that held the hound's ears on the back of its neck while eating. He soon found many other long-haired spaniel owners interested in his invention, so he offered it to a small manufacturer who produced it and now markets it in pet stores around the country. His royalties will keep the cocker in bones for a long time to come.

IDEAS THAT BUILD IMAGE

Perhaps even more important to 20th Century man than food, clothing, shelter and transportation, is the need for recognition. As the age of the computer, the credit card, governmentalization, and industrialization categorizes him and substitutes numbers for his name, he stands in real danger of losing his identity as an individual. For today's man, the dangers of atomic war, over-population, and pollution are often secondary to the increasing possibility that he may soon become little more than a 12-digit number in a complex computer-dominated world. Give him ideas that help assure his fame and popularity, that will set him apart from the earth's other four billion inhabitants, and he will be glad to pay for your ideas.

Advertisers have been impressed with the results of recent mail order campaigns in which the recipient's name, address, and other pertinent facts about him or his neighborhood are included two or three times throughout the advertising message. This method, accomplished by a simple taping device, was the brainchild of a corporation executive who felt that the many pieces of junk mail addressed to "boxholder" or "occupant" were an insult to the consumer's identity and caused more ill will than sales.

Seeing one's own name in print is both a morale and an ego booster, and ideas which offer a man the opportunity for fame, no matter how fleeting, will always be worth money to their creator.

HOW CREATIVE ARE YOU? was the theme of a contest in Salt Lake City, sponsored by a major manufacturer of cellophane tape. In a full-page ad featuring an assortment of humorous eyes, ears, noses, mustaches, toupees, etc., the company offered cash prizes for the most creative faces (stuck together, of course, with their cellophane tape). In addition, the winners' names would be published in a subsequent ad in the same newspapers. It turned out to be the firm's most successful promotion—a complete sellout of the product throughout the city, plus more than 60 times the number of entries they had expected. They discovered people were even more interested in getting their names published as "creative winners" than in the cash prizes—although they gladly accepted those, too.

While there are numerous ways to appeal to a man's basic need for "image," one of the most effective is price. If your idea contains some real or imaginary prestige factor, and is expensive enough, you may have a winner. Look:

What started as a publicity gimmick turned out to be one of the hottest items in a Texas department store recently. It's called an Executive Sandbox—a real sandbox, designed for the office. It is billed as the "latest relief for the tense businessman" and an "excellent plaything." An amazingly large number of these "playthings" were sold—at $456.00 each! Its inventor then put his COMPACT REDUCER device to work to come up with a popular-priced version. He's now selling these for $15 all over the country.

Companies, too, large or small, know they must have a "good image" to be well thought of by their customers and their stockholders. They willingly spend large sums of money for image-builders such as charitable or educational foundations, industrial museums, parks, stadiums, buildings, athletic teams, and the like. Offer them something that will help them build a good image, and it can be worth money to you.

An attic "treasure" led to a sale by a 72-year old woman. She discovered some old books on household remedies which were worth only a few dollars as antiques. She felt they should be worth more—to somebody. So she borrowed a trade journal from a local pharmacist, obtained a list of all the large drug firms, and sent letters of inquiry to each to see if they would be interested in the books. One large firm wrote back that they would like the books to display in their historical library—and included a check for $50 in payment.

IDEAS FOR PLEASURE

The pursuit of pleasure is one of today's biggest businesses and it promises to become bigger. For some idea of just how valuable 20th Century man considers his pleasure to be, you need only look at what he's willing to pay the great entertainers—movie stars, TV personalities, professional athletes, playwrights, etc. There's money to be made in helping man enjoy himself. All it takes is an idea.

A man pays $1.50 in a Playboy Club for a drink he could buy at Jake's Bar for 50¢—because of the more appealing "trimmings" in the Playboy Club. He pays $15 for seats to a pro football game he could have watched on TV—because of the stimulation of a large, excited crowd. He pays $1,000 for membership in a country club when he could play golf at a municipal course for a third of that—because of the pleasant atmosphere of the clubhouse and the companionship of its members. He pays $5,000 for a lifetime membership in a class which teaches him the latest dance steps which his teenage nieces would gladly teach him for free—because of the chance for social contact and congenial atmosphere he finds in the class. He pays thousands for yachts, private planes, diving equipment, summer cottages, winter resorts, overseas vacations, stamp collections, art objects, etc.

Why? Because these things have been beautifully "wrapped" in an idea and sold as a more exciting way of living.

Mix *your* creative ideas for pleasure with generous portions of your *time, talent,* or *treasure,* and see the profitable opportunities that arise. Giving pleasure is one thing, but turning drudgery into pleasure is another, and if your idea can do that, it's worth money! Take the case of the unusual laundromats:

> Ronald Gill was discussing his latest investment with a friend. "Nothing very exciting—just a string of coin-operated laundromats," he said. "But why shouldn't they be exciting?" his friend replied. "An establishment doesn't have to be dull and routine just because it performs a useful function." The two men began brainstorming ways to liven up laundromats. The result: a combination coin laundry and discothèque. At the door, attendants dressed in bunny-like costumes take cutsomers' dirty clothes and put them in the washer for a small fee. While the clothes are washing, the customer can loosen up at the laundry's bar with $1-drinks, or relax on its dance floor. For singles who want to mix, booths and snack bar are available. What started out on a small scale is now on its way to becoming a large franchise operation —and a profitable one.

People love beauty, and they are willing to pay to surround themselves with it—at home, at work, in their places of worship or entertainment. But their tastes change, and the dynamic person must be alert to new ways to inspire the beauty-lover. Look how one woman converted a common, ordinarily worthless item into a beautiful "treasure" for which people were willing to pay.

> While driving through northern Ohio in the early summer, Jane Talley was captivated by the vast array of colorful weeds along the roadsides. On impulse she stopped and picked a bouquet and made it into an attractive arrangement. She used it as a table decoration at a party she was giving that evening. She received not only many compliments, but also requests from friends for similar arrangements. She followed through with "weed expeditions" in which she picked large quantities of weeds, dried them, and sprayed some with paint to give them a greater variety of colors. She rented a booth in a local antique festival in which she sold not only arrangements, but also the dried weeds themselves in bulk form from which purchasers could make their own assortments. It was the most popular booth at the fair, and by far the most profitable since the "inventory" had been free for the taking.

Take advantage of time and circumstances. Timing is everything to certain ideas, so take action on your idea when the time is right—because it may not return again for a long time.

In Cleveland, a particularly severe snowstorm hit around mid-morning after all the employees of a large supermarket had already arrived for work. The day's business dropped to nothing, and after the clerks had stocked the shelves and cleaned the store, they had nothing to do. The owner, who was in the store at the time, said "Everybody outside—we're going to make snowballs." He called the other stores in the chain and commanded the same thing. The thousands of snowballs made by the employees that day were put into a deep freezer where they remained until July, when the owner promoted a "snowballs in July" super sale, featuring supervised "snowball fights" among children in the parking lot, and a "free December snowball" to every customer—as a reminder during the heat wave that cooler days were ahead. Customers enjoyed the unseasonable but pleasurable interlude, and sales volume rose to an all-time high during the three-day snowball sale.

If you have talent that can give others pleasure, put it to use—profitable use. If you can develop a unique "schtick" for it to make you unique from others with similar talents, so much the better. Look at the Beatles, Tiny Tim, and countless others who simply added a touch of the bizarre to their talent to give some added pleasure. It paid for them—handsomely.

Mal Chambers wanted to go to college some six years after he had graduated from high school, but was unable to pay for it. He had taken some lessons in square dancing, so he decided to become a professional caller and use that money to pay his way. He perked up the dances he called for by composing many of his own tunes and calls, and soon became a favorite among square-dance buffs. By the time he finished college, he estimated he had called for over 40,000 people in a four-year period. To celebrate his graduation, and to thank those who helped him pay for it, he took out a half-page ad in a monthly square-dancer's magazine and announced his free "diploma dance." Some 400 avid square dancers showed up to accept his unique "thank you."

Don't fall back on the I CAN'T POSSIBLY DO THAT mental crutch just because your talents aren't on the grand scale of public entertainers. This is true of most of us. There is *something* you can do—many things, probably. Take a few moments to list what you do best and what you enjoy doing. Then determine who might be willing to pay for those talents. You'll be surprised to find you have many ways of converting your creative ability to a marketable product. Look at these two homespun examples:

> The Wilson family has spent the last ten summers in a rented cottage on Cape Cod because of the spare-time talents of Mrs. Wilson. Each day she makes a large batch of fudge which one member of the family sells from a card table along the road in front of the cottage. This "Cape Cod Fudge" has become so popular that many tourists come from all over the cape to buy it. The income from Mrs. Wilson's fudge more than pays for the family's summer vacations.
>
> The decorations committee for a woman's club banquet decided to do something different. So they bought plastic flowers, dipped them in a varnish mixture, and made individual Flemish floral arrangements for favors. The arrangements were a hit, and women began placing orders for more. So the committee gals went into the business of dipping and making arrangements for profit. In a year's time they had netted several hundred dollars apiece.

Public speaking can be a good source of income. While it requires some speaking ability, the most important thing is to have a good story to tell. Do you have a special talent, interest, or unique hobby which others would like to hear about? It can be worth money.

> Alicia Penn is a "hat nut." Ever since she was a teenager, she has worn hats everywhere regardless of the occasion. This in itself isn't unusual, but Alicia never disposes of a hat. She has every one she ever owned—over 100 in all—kept in a special walk-in closet designed by her husband. Now she gives talks on her hats to women's groups, appealing to their sense of nostalgia as she tries on various models from the "good old days," giving a brief history of each. Her earnings from the talks helps support her insatiable "hat habit."

IDEAS THAT PROVIDE A SERVICE

In our age of affluence, basic needs are satisfied rather quickly; thus "service" becomes an important item to thousands of individuals, organizations, businesses, and even countries. Have you an idea that will serve someone, or a group of someones? It could be valuable to a large number of people, or it might simply be a helping hand to a few individuals. In either case, it can be worth money.

Many a worthwhile service or serviceable invention came about as the result of creative problem solving. As you solve the immediate problem facing you, step back from the results and ask yourself, "Who else might have a similar problem and might benefit from a similar solution?" If the answer is "plenty of people," you may have a salable idea. It paid off for these two dynamic personalities:

William Bowman, a mechanical engineering student, spent two summers working in a locksmith's shop in California where he learned to master the intricacies of the lock and key. He also worked as a part-time fireman in the nearby town during the school year. He began reflecting on the numerous complaints leveled against firemen about the damage they cause when breaking into a burning building. He applied his knowledge of locks to the problem and came up with an unusual door opener which pushes door jams apart, allowing the latch to slip out of its catch so the door can be pushed open easily. Damage to door frames is negligible, especially when compared to the damage caused by a fireman's axe. The device was enthusiastically received by fire chiefs around the country. Bill has opened the door to other promising commercial possibilities with his door-opener.

Marsden Ellis was frustrated because he was unable to write to a blind friend without enlisting the services of a Braille typist. To him it didn't make sense that a person should have to know Braille in order to write a blind person, so he set about adapting a standard electric typewriter with which anyone who could type could type Braille, thus making the advantage of Braille available to far more people. He worked on the project during his spare time for nearly three years before perfecting such a machine. His first act was to write his blind friend a letter. His second was to take his prototype to his firm and propose that they manufacture it. They did—and today Braille typewriters are available all over the country.

Observing the frustrations of others, too, can be the springboard to good ideas. Here's an instance:

> Ralph Kennedy listened to the girls at his office complain about the many duplicate gifts they received at showers, many of which could not be returned or exchanged. So he applied the creative principle of substitution to start a part-time business. He substituted "swapping" for buying. He opened a small shop in Cleveland and stocked it with everything from toys to appliances and some very strange household and personal items. These things are not for sale, but he will trade them for something of similar value. He charges a small fee for the service. He does a booming business around Christmas, as well as at "shower time."

Take advantage of a timely situation. The moment for making money with an idea may come and go if you're not thinking imaginatively all the time. Take the case of the helpful pretzel vendor:

> Several visitors appeared stranded at Grand Central Terminal in New York, vainly trying to hail a taxi during the rush hours. A vendor with a pretzel car saw their plight and offered to let them put their 13 pieces of luggage on his cart while he pushed it for them to their hotel three blocks away. They accepted gratefully and rewarded him with a handsome tip for the use of his "vehicle."

Naturally, not every idea will be a winner—at least not for everyone concerned. Occasionally a creative idea can be "un-done" by other creative-thinking people, as happened in the case of an Indianapolis radio station recently:

> As a publicity gimmick, the station offered a five-cent bounty on every mosquito brought into the studio by its listeners. The publicity people estimated the promotion would cost $100 or so. They were completely dismayed when contestants brought in a total of 225,481 mosquitoes—and hit the station up for $11,274.05. One especially imaginative housewife located a breeding ground near her home which she bug-bombed. She collected 73,225 of the insects, and received a reluctant $3,661.25 for her efforts!

IDEAS THAT ENHANCE PEOPLE'S PERSONAL POWER

Since the days many years ago when Dale Carnegie promised to make public speakers out of wallflowers and Charles Atlas promised to turn 98-pound weaklings into dynamic musclemen (and made a fortune in the process), Americans have spent billions of dollars on improving their mental, social, or physical capabilities. Forecasters for the decade of the 1970's claim that this will remain one of the highest priorities on nearly everyone's list.

Consider how you can combine your time, talents and treasure with creative thinking to provide people with greater personal power. If your talent can help another person develop his talent, you have a salable commodity. If it is in a specialized field, so much the better, because there are always those who are interested in learning it—and willing to pay for the lessons.

Chuck Gilbert, a greeting card editor and writer, was concerned about the number of people who submitted ideas to card companies and "just missed" because of a lack of knowledge about the market, not a lack of talent on the writer's part. So he began a "learn-by-mail" writing service for would-be card writers, featuring market information as well as tips on writing. Enrollment jumped to several hundred persons, and he was able to supplement his income by several thousand dollars a year helping others help themselves.

Many talented people—artists, craftsmen, dramatists, etc.—earn extra money teaching their "thing" in adult education classes and other special schools. What's *your* special talent? If you can add to a person's physical strength, or eliminate a problem that comes from not having a certain amount of strength when it's needed most—you have a salable idea.

When his wife came home one evening with a long tale of frustration and woe which began with a flat tire she was unable to fix on a busy highway, Marvin Wentworth started thinking of ways to build a better jack—one which a woman, even the most frail, could operate with ease. It had to be light, easy to handle, and practically foolproof. One evening he watched his little boy give his teddy bear a "ride" by inflating a large balloon beneath it. Marvin had an idea, and he put the ALL-PURPOSE ADAPTER technique to work immediately. The result was an inflatable car jack made of rubber which inflates in less than a minute, using compressed air or gas, and which lifts the flat wheel some three inches off the ground. A large manufacturer bought the concept immediately, recognizing the value of substituting "air power" for muscle power.

"A thing is worth whatever the buyer will pay for it," says an old Roman proverb which still holds true today. Every idea has some value, depending upon its nature and to which of man's six basic needs it is directed. The more widespread its use, however, the more valuable it will be, and conversely, the more limited the application of an idea, the less salable it is.

If your pet hamster falls down a well and you quickly invent a device for extracting him, you've provided a worthwhile service— but on a onetime basis. Not many hamsters fall down wells and need rescuing by a concerned owner, so your creative invention served a useful purpose but is simply not commercially usable. On the other hand, if your invention would extract *anything* that might fall into a well, you have something commercially salable to well-owners to make your well-retrieving device a million-dollar idea. If, however, the same extraction device could be adapted for universal use in industry, by homeowners, by farmers, etc., you suddenly have a "mass market" item—and something that is worth money.

Test each of your ideas against a potential market. If you've done something clever to solve a very specific problem or just for your own amusement, put your creative tools to work in considering a broader application for it. Can you add to it—enlarge it—make it smaller—make it cheaper—or adapt it in some other way to make it more valuable? If you can, you have a salable idea. If not—well, try again! After all, there are plenty more ideas where that one came from—right?

IDEAS FOR INCREASING YOUR INCOME

Let's start by providing yourself with some good reasons why you *want* to increase your income. Take a sheet of paper and jot down a dozen things you've wanted to do "If I only had the money." Now list a dozen things you have which you consider valuable. They may be your ideas, your product, your time, etc. If it's ideas, list them specifically.

Compare the list you've made with the six basics we discussed in this chapter and put numbers next to each item as it meets these, as follows: (1) *Make him more money;* (2) *serve his basic needs;* (3) *build his image;* (4) *give him pleasure;* (5) *provide a worthwhile service;* (6) *enhance his personal power.* Are your ideas suitable?

Pick your "pet" idea from this group and list all the ways you can think of to sell it. Do the same with other ideas from your list.

8

Settling for Nothing Less Than Success

There aren't any rules for success that work unless you do.

Anon.

Not long ago, at a meeting in which leaders from nearly every type of business were gathered, the representatives of a dozen major industries were discussing their most urgent needs for the decade. Some of their actual statements are revealing of a present attitude toward the dynamic creative individual in today's business world:

"The dynamic man can write his own ticket in business today!"

"One creative person is worth a dozen computers in any corporation!"

"I don't need a company—I need a man and an idea!"

"One idea from one man grossed this firm over eight million dollars this year . . . we could use plenty like him!"

"If we had even one creative individual in each department, we could double our efficiency and our business! Believe me, they're as scarce as diamonds!"

"A creative person in the retail world stands out like the statue of liberty—and is just as welcome!"

"The man who's always ready with an idea is far more valuable than a man who's always right!"

"The dynamic individual makes business a pleasure—for himself and his employer!"

"The creative man is a pain in the you-know-where—always disrupting things!"

These executives were (almost) unanimous in their recognition that dynamic "idea people" are the most valuable asset their organizations can have. The old success gimmicks, once considered surefire during the first two-thirds of this century—shrewd dealing, office politics, apple polishing, eyewash, being a personality kid, outshouting the other guy, and out-and-out ruthlessness—won't carry you very far in today's business world. It's a world of sophistication and "bottom line" philosophies where results are the real measurements of a man's worth.

You *can* succeed in today's complex business world. To do so is going to require some creative effort from you—some *consistent* effort not just to come up with ideas for new products or marketing concepts, but to improve every phase of your work. First, determine just what you want to do, and how far you want to go, then devote the bulk of your time and efforts to improving yourself in these four critical areas:

1. *Creativity.* Be a totally creative person on the job from 9 to 5—and then some. Be an idea man in small things as well as large. Use your imagination to get the job you want—then keep it. Set idea goals (one a day—two a day?) then better them. Don't rely on luck but make good use of it when it comes your way.

2. *Craftmanship.* Become an expert in your field. If you can't work harder, work smarter! Make your shortcuts creative. Use creative methods to become a real "pro." Sell yourself by demonstrating your ability!

3. *Consideration.* Be loyal to your company, your boss, your co-workers and your customers. Be thoughtful of others, even though it sometimes requires a lot of effort. Be a good leader or a good follower—or both. Respect time and use it wisely.

4. *Confidence.* Have faith in your ability. Tackle anything, but tackle it creatively. Don't be afraid of fear and treat failure as a friend. Question the system, but be positive,

not negative. And be willing to make a job change, if necessary.

A job will always be just a job if you treat it as merely something that occupies eight or so hours of your time daily and provides you with a paycheck at the end of the week. But if you approach it with enthusiasm and all the creative devices at your disposal, it can be an exciting, fulfilling, and rewarding experience. Become a creative craftsman—considerate and confident!

CREATIVITY

A dramatic indication of the vital need for dynamic people and new ideas in industry is a statement made by the president of the Du Pont corporation in a recent stockholders' meeting:

Seventy-five per cent of our sales dollars this year came from products that we didn't even know existed ten years ago!

This is from a company whose volume exceeds two billion dollars a year. In other words, new ideas will account for over 1.5 billion dollars worth of business this year—in just one company alone!

What can *your ideas* mean to *your company* this year? They're badly needed, you know, both for your sake and the company's. The creativity you show on your job today will make all the difference in where you will be five or ten years from now—and certainly in how much money you will be making.

Be an idea man, not an alibi expert. Your employer wants solutions, not problems, from you. Forget your mental crutches. Instead of listing a dozen reasons why "it can't be done," list 25 ways it *can* be done. You needn't spend pages of reports describing the difficulty of the problem; the boss probably knew it was difficult when he asked for your help with it. Give him an idea, not an alibi.

A Chicago taxi company asked its drivers for suggestions on improving business. Many of the responses were of a sarcastic or negative nature, but one enterprising driver presented a list of 25 ideas. Some were practical, some far-fetched, but he submitted them all. Number 24 on the list was "Install TV sets for passengers to watch." To his surprise, the company went for the idea, saying they felt riders would welcome something different. They installed five-inch screens in 100 of their cabs. The result: Passengers were pleased and many went out of their way to select that company's cabs for their ride. The drivers, too, were pleased to report receiving bigger tips.

Don't rely on the old mental crutch THAT'S NOT MY RESPONSIBILITY. Suggest ideas even in areas that "don't concern" you. Remember, you prosper only if your company prospers. Look at the example of how an alibi expert closed his eyes to an expensive goof on the part of his employer.

An oil equipment firm employed a consultant to help them reduce excessive costs in their operation. On one of his observation trips the consultant went to the railroad yard and watched the loading of long lengths of oil piping onto flatbed cars. He noticed that the workmen were using Grade A white pine as spacers between the pipes. He asked the foreman why this expensive wood was being used and the foreman replied, "That's not my responsibility! The Purchasing Department does the buying —I just use what they buy for me." The consultant went to the purchasing agent who agreed at once to buy a cheaper grade wood. The change resulted in a saving of $48,000 in one year.

Set an "idea goal" for yourself. Then map a course to help you accomplish it. An idea a day is a good, realistic goal—for a start. Can you imagine how much you could accomplish on your job, with your company, in your store, in your laboratory, at your drawing board, at your typewriter, with an idea a day? That's over 300 ideas a year! If even a third of these turn out to be good, usable ideas, think what a contribution you will make—both to your employer and your own sense of satisfaction.

Then next year, double your goal, or triple it, and watch the results! Be a *real* leader. Inspire those working for you to try an idea a day, and you'll find you've generated a tremendously powerful creative force—and an effective one, too!

At the end of each year, the editor of a large publication has his managers list their goals for the coming year, complete with suggestions as to how they plan to accomplish them. He then incorporates these into a master "direction book" which outlines projects and priorities for an entire year. On the first working day of the new year, the editor distributes and discusses these books with all his employees so that everyone knows what they are expected to accomplish in the coming 12 months. Progress is checked quarterly and new fires lit under slow-moving projects, and at year's end, a final report is made. Last year, the managers proudly reported that 100% of the year's objectives had been accomplished.

Be creative by plan, not accident. Luck, as we've discussed previously, plays an important role in the creation of new ideas and products, and you should be alert to capitalize on it. But the employer or employee who merely sits around waiting for luck or inspiration to strike may find himself receiving his gold retirement watch before receiving that first luck idea. Use your SYSTEMATIC SEARCHER frequently. *Plan* your creative efforts. Take steps to *force* luck to come your way.

An employee of a chemical company was walking home via the nearby city dump. He was beset by millions of flies, but as he came to a particular spot in the dump, there were no flies at all. It was like an oasis in the desert and it aroused his curiosity. He discovered that the area was saturated with a substance his company had dumped there—a substance which not only resisted flies, but seemed to drive them away with a vengeance. He took a sample to work the next day, turned it over to the chemical engineers, and in a few months the company had a new insecticide. The employee received a bonus—but the engineers and management received a reprimand from their president. "Why," he asked, "should we have to rely on chance accidents to build our business? We need a definite, positive plan for developing new business products!" Included in the subsequent plan of action were chemical analyses of all waste products before dumping, and weekly field trips for chemical engineers—including occasional visits to the city dump!

CRAFTSMANSHIP

The way to earn more is to be worth more! Use your dynamic personality to make yourself valuable. Learn your job well, then do it well—better, in fact, than anyone might reasonably expect you to do it.

Work hard. It isn't always a popular concept today, but it's an effective one. The very fact that we live in a work-shy age means that the dynamic energetic person can more easily make his way toward the success he seeks.

Think smarter. Always be alert to creative ways to do your job better—or to strengthen your ability to do your job.

Use every opportunity to demonstrate your ability. Be sure those who can reward you have plenty of chances to see just what you can do. Don't be satisfied with "average" or "well enough." Mediocre performances will always command mediocre wages; mediocre recognition will result in nothing but a mediocre future. Be outstanding in your field—a real craftsman!

Keep up to date! Know what's going on within your company, your industry, your market. Don't rely on the old crutch NOBODY TELLS ME ANYTHING! Be interested enough to find out on your own.

> Told he was being released after ten years with the company, John Riley expressed surprise. "Why would you terminate anyone with ten years' experience?" he asked his boss. "That's just the trouble" was the reply, "you don't have ten years' experience —you have one year's experience repeated ten times. You don't keep up with the changing times. You still do everything just as you did ten years ago. Look at Paul Downs—he's always up-to-date on everything concerning this business, and he's always coming up with suggestions for improvements and new methods."
>
> John related his tale of woe to Paul and asked his secret. Paul's "secret" was a simple thing—one that cost him about $12 a year and a little reading time! He subscribed to the three leading trade journals of his industry, and made periodic visits to the library to browse through those of other industries. He was constantly getting ideas from these sources which were applicable to his particular job. And, he always made sure his boss was aware of them.

Think job! Ignore the old admonitions "Don't take the job home with you," and "Don't talk shop." They are uncreative and unproductive for the dynamic craftsman. You improve a skill by using that skill, not by letting it lie in disuse half the time. When you're off the job, "think job." Not the worries, frustrations or problems of the job, but the skills, the product, and the market for that product. Keep your SYSTEMATIC SEARCHER working all the time. Observe your customers and learn more about them. Look for ideas that relate to your job no matter where you are or what you're doing.

On his way to work one morning, Dick Stensrude, a greeting card writer, observed a house that was in the process of being demolished for a freeway. "Wow," he said jokingly to the rest of the car pool, "what a party they must've had last night!" When he arrived at work, he requested a staff photographer who took several shots of the partly wrecked home. For the finished photo, he wrote a gag, "Thanks—I had a real blast at your party!" which was accepted and used, and which became a best-seller.

Be a professional—a dynamic one! Think, act, talk and *work* like one. Approach your vocation with the enthusiasm and dedication it deserves. Use your creative machinery to help you live up to this definition of a "real pro" which a publisher recently distributed to all his employees:

What Is a Pro?

The next time there's an important job to be done, take a good long look at who is selected to handle it. Chances are, he's a professional—a real pro. Chances are, too, he'll do the job right—because that's the way a pro performs.

A pro is someone who knows where he is going, why he is going, and how he intends to get there. He enjoys his work because he does it well; he does it well because he enjoys it.

He's someone who is always ready with a good idea when it's needed most—plus a few dozen more nobody even asked for. He's someone who worked hard to get where he is—and still hasn't lost the hard work habit.

A pro is someone whose enthusiasm is catching.

He's realistic enough to know he's going to make mistakes—but intelligent enough not to make the same one twice.

He's honest enough to admit defeat, mature enough to shrug off discouragement, and tenacious enough to try again—and again. He's discriminating enough to distinguish the important from the petty—but thoughtful enough to accept both as something to be dealt with.

A pro is a dreamer, but even with his head in the clouds, his feet are always on the ground.

He takes concern over small things—but refuses to let small things worry him.

He knows how to lead without being dictatorial and how to follow without kowtowing. When he's leading, he develops leaders under him; when he's following, he does his best to make his leaders successful.

He doesn't wait till someone motivates him—because he motivates himself.

A pro is creative but not eccentric; daring, but not reckless; dedicated, but not fanatic.

A pro is someone who gets things done. Thank God he exists!

CONSIDERATION

Nice guys *do* get ahead—and for a reason. When you're enthusiastic, considerate, honest and loyal you're going to get plenty of help from above *and* below. When you're a leader with these qualities, those under you will be more than willing to give you a boost. When you're a follower, those over you will help you up, because they need dependable, trustworthy people. If you're in business for yourself, your customers will help you because they, too, are grateful when they find someone with whom they feel comfortable.

Show those around you that you appreciate them and their position. Be quick with a compliment and slow with a criticism.

Respect time, both your own and that of others. Don't waste it, use it creatively. When you use those last few minutes before quitting time by coming up with an idea instead of putting on your hat and coat, you're telling your employer "I like you—and I'm doing my best for you."

Be polite and tactful. Don't shout or show your anger. If you have a quick temper, devise a creative method of controlling it, whether it be counting to ten or simply walking away.

Be patient, even when it hurts. A dynamic person hasn't the time to waste being negative in response to negative people.

A customer was being particularly obnoxious to the department store clerk, but was receiving only courteous, gentle responses in return. When the angry customer finally left, a fellow-clerk asked, "Why didn't you just tell her off?" The clerk shrugged and replied, "It wouldn't have solved anything. Anyhow, I feel if she can stand herself 24 hours a day, I can certainly stand her for a few minutes."

Have the right attitude. Maintain a cheerful, optimistic approach to your work and you'll accomplish three things: you'll enjoy your work more, you'll influence those around you in a positive, constructive way, and you'll impress the hell out of your employer. He doesn't have many like you!

> A newspaper reporter, after a rather hectic interview, glanced at the sunlight as he stepped into a waiting taxi. "It's too beautiful a day to work," he said to the driver. "What do you mean!" the driver exclaimed, "This is the kind of day you love to work!" After that, it was.

Be loyal! Your employer has enough problems facing him without having to be worried about what's going on behind his back. Elbert Hubbard put it this way:

> If you work for a man, in Heaven's name, *work* for him. If he pays you wages which supply your bread and butter, work for him; speak well of him; stand by him and stand by the institution he represents. If put to a pinch, an ounce of loyalty is worth a pound of cleverness. If you must vilify, resign your position; but as long as you are a part of the institution, do not condemn it.

This doesn't mean you must accept the status quo come what may. You should use your creative ability to improve any operation and to correct legitimate grievances, but in a positive, constructive way. Do more than just point out problems—suggest improvements! When others criticize your company, your product, your co-workers, or your boss, say something good in response. Whenever the opportunity arises, show your employer you're behind him—come what may.

> Whenever Tyler Yates takes a new job, he immediately buys $100 worth of stock in that company. He explains: "This makes me feel more a part of the company. Its problems become my problems even if on a smaller scale. I find myself more honestly concerned about its profits. I also find myself feeling more a part of the team when I receive shareholders' reports. Perhaps most important, I consider it a gesture of loyalty to my new employer.

It's my way of saying 'I believe in you and I'm backing you to the best of my ability!' "

Follow through! Be open to suggestions from your employer or employees and follow through on them. If a suggestion is valueless, you may lose some time and effort, but the person suggesting it will know you were interested enough to react to his idea. If it's a good one, you'll increase his confidence in himself and you. Be willing to innovate; add your own creative touch to the suggestion.

Acting upon a suggestion from his boss, Marshall Bullard enrolled in a marketing class to supplement his field experience. He proceeded to demonstrate to his employer that it was a good idea by circulating to his co-workers and boss a weekly two-page boil-down of what he had learned during the week. He titled it "What's New in Marketing?" He also copied articles on topical subjects, underlining those items of greatest interest, and sent them to the boss with notations like "Maybe we should consider this approach." He selected a problem to tackle in his semester paper that had been plaguing his company. Using his ideas and some from his professor, he presented the company with several possible solutions, one of which the company modified slightly and put into action. "Graduation Day" was followed by a raise and increased responsibilities for Marshall.

Ask for suggestions and help! When you're planning a change, be sure it's really needed. Check whether or not the old way might not work just as well as the new. Ask those who do the work for their suggestions and ideas. Tell them what you need—not what you demand. You'll not only get results, you'll be showing them you have confidence in them.

Jack McKittrick, head of a systems team, was called to review a new purchase order checking method installed in a store some three weeks earlier. When he asked the store superintendent how things were going, the answer was "Fine! We've already cut 12 hours off the merchandise processing time!" This seemed too good to be true so soon after a new system was installed, so the team returned to the checking area and asked each person to tell what they were doing now and what they did under the old method. It became quickly apparent there was no difference in what they were doing; they hadn't yet switched to the new method! So Jack asked the supervisor to explain how he had cut 12 hours of processing time. He replied, "Well, management told us they were going to change to the purchase-order method to knock about 12 hours off our processing time. We didn't like the new method, so we decided to give them what they wanted without changing anything!"

CONFIDENCE

Self-confidence can accomplish two important things for you as a dynamic person: It will provide you with the strength to persevere in your work, and it will inspire others to trust you—your abilities, your judgement, and perhaps more important, the value of your ideas. If you have faith in yourself, you'll find it easier to convince others to have faith in you. Show your self-confidence through your ability to solve problems creatively, to set others at ease, to disregard the fears and doubts that can drive you up a wall if you allow them.

Get rid of fear—it's uncreative! Perhaps the most frequently given reason for not suggesting or following through on an idea is "I'm afraid." The greatest worry-wart of all time was Chicken Little, who feared the sky was falling. He kept the barnyard in a turmoil with his fretting and finally caused not only his own destruction, but also that of many of his barnyard friends. Our fears are often just as groundless. We worry about what "they" will think or say; that it will cause us to lose money; that "I'll do the wrong thing"; or worst of all, "I'll lose my job!"

To succeed at anything, you must take a chance. If you review all the reasons why you shouldn't try something new, chances are you'll *never* try it. If you list the ways it *can* be done, you'll find a way to accomplish it.

One dynamic executive applies a simple formula to anything he finds himself fearing to tackle. He asks himself, "What's the worst that can possibly happen?" As he answers his fears this way, they no longer seem so formidable. Ridicule? The loss of a few dollars? Someone's anger? Losing a job? He knows none of these are fatal. "Many times," he says, "I've decided the worst that could happen was easily worth the risk of success. It's paid off—handsomely."

View failure as a teacher, not an executioner. One of the first and most important steps toward succeeding in anything is to discard your fear of failure. Failure is not disgraceful. On the contrary, failure is often a sign of creativeness! Even a plain out-and-out complete failure offers you a certain dignity because it is evidence to the fact that you have at least *tried* to do something.

A young executive handed his boss a letter of resignation, citing two recent dismal flops as evidence of his unfitness for the job. The boss asked, "Would you consider as a failure, a baseball player who struck out 1330 times during his career?" The young man said he would. "And how about a pitcher who lost 433 games?" "Another failure," the man responded. "Well," said the boss, "the man who struck out 1330 times was Babe Ruth—but he's only remembered for his 714 home runs. And the pitcher was Cy Young, who won 511 games while losing those 433. Before you're through in this business, you'll have a long list of failures behind you—but you'll have your successes too, and that's what counts. Failure just plain doesn't matter, except as a guidepost for yourself. Now tear this letter up and get back to work!" Twelve years later the young man was named vice president of his firm.

Be fair. Allow others their failures, too. Be quick to praise the success and accomplishments of others, but be the last to ridicule their failures. Rather, offer your help for the next "go-around." The words "Can I help?" will carry you much further than "I told you so!"

Use your imagination to get the job you want! If there's little or no hope of finding creative fulfillment in your present occupation, make a change! Easier said than done? Perhaps, but with determination and an imaginative approach, you can land the job you want. Here are some ideas. Add more of your own—then go ahead and land the big one!

Dig! Don't go job-hunting "cold turkey." Select a firm you're interested in, then find out all you can about it—its product, its production methods, its market, its personnel policies, its management. If it's a public-held corporation, look up the annual report and get the feel of the company's philosophy. Pick up some catch words to use in the interview to show you've done your homework. Prepare a creative resume. Don't just mimeograph a hundred copies of your working history in the same format used by five million other job seekers. Draw upon your creative power tools to help you do something different, even if it's no more than putting things down on a different-colored paper. Try an illustrated resume, or one in book form, or one that's larger, or smaller. Whatever you do, make it look professional—one your prospective employer will remember. If you're in a middle management job, you should prepare for your job switch in advance by making yourself known in your field. This you can accomplish several ways:

> Attend meetings of professional groups in your industry. Accept opportunities to speak at industry gatherings. Contribute articles to trade papers read by those who are potential employers. Above all maintain a flexible occupational outlook. Make job changing part of your overall career plan, not just a matter of meeting occupational crises.

If the job you're seeking is your first, it's even more important to use a creative approach. Remember, to the employer you're an unknown, with only a scholastic record to speak for you (and sometimes that may not speak well). Think of ways you can give your name added meaning to the interviewer. Here's how one enterprising job-seeker did it:

> Phil Donelli, just graduating college, realized he was up against a lot of competition for the job in which he was most interested —that of a sales engineer for one of the major steel concerns. He was graduating from one of the smallest and least-known colleges in Ohio and had never done any selling. In fact, he wasn't even sure he would like the job, but decided to find out. He wrote a letter to the vice-president of sales. He didn't ask for the job— merely for the opportunity to travel with one of the experienced salesmen for three days to discover for himself what was required of a sales engineer. Because his letter was different from the approximately 400 other letters the company received, he got the interview, the chance to travel with the salesman—and the job!

Once you find *the* job, and you've determined it's right for you, give it all you've got. Work at it—and work hard! Think at it— give it your best ideas! Be a craftsman—the best in your field! Be confident—in yourself and in those you work for and with. Be considerate—of your employer, your employees, your customers— of everyone with whom you come in contact! And, perhaps most important of all, be creative! Use your imagination and ideas to help you succeed! An idea a day and you're on your way—right to the top!

IDEAS FOR A MORE SUCCESSFUL YOU

Sit down and put your IDEA GENERATOR to work. On a sheet of paper, list under each of the categories below a dozen (or more) ideas by which you can become stronger and more successful in your chosen field: *How can I be more creative? How can I become a better craftsman? How can I better show my consideration? How can I build my self-confidence?*

Once you have your lists, don't close the book on them. Put them to work today! The sooner you start, the faster you can move!

9

How to Become Proficient at Selling—
Especially Selling Ideas!

> *Selling is easy if you work hard enough at it.*
> Jacob M. Braude

Every dynamic person is a salesman, although not every salesman is a dynamic person. The ability to sell creatively is a vital talent that you, as an "idea man," must develop and improve. Many a good idea has died a-borning or has gathered dust for months, years, or even generations because its creator wasn't inventive enough in presenting and selling his idea. The zipper, for example, was invented in 1879, but was so strongly and effectively opposed by button manfacturers that it wasn't marketed until some 30 years later.

Regardless of your occupation, you, then, must be a salesman—an idea salesman with the same kind of faith in and enthusiasm for your ideas that a top-notch salesman has for his company and his product. You must have an awareness of the selling process as well as the required skills, determination, perseverance, patience and creativity it requires.

Think modern! Don't rely on the world beating a path to your doorstep when you build a better mousetrap. It may have been good philosophy a hundred years ago when it was first uttered, but the 20th Century simply doesn't operate that way. Today even the world's best mousetrap has to be sold—and so must even the best ideas.

The mere fact that your idea is good, practical, economical, profitable, and badly needed is not enough to get it off the ground. You must be able to *prove* those things to someone else's complete satisfaction. In fact, there will usually be more than one "someone else" involved in placing the final yes or no on your ideas. If you know these people and understand them and their thinking processes, you stand a far better chance of selling them than if you approach them "cold turkey."

Let's take a moment, then, to meet the "committee" which will be most frequently called upon to review and approve your ideas. No doubt you've already run into many of them when you were involved in previous selling jobs; rest assured that the more good ideas you come up with in the future, the more of these "committee members" you're going to meet.

SUSPICIOUS SAM	— He suspects your idea simply because it's new and he knows "new" may mean a higher casualty rate and more expense than "old." He's doubtful as to whether you've worked out all the possible bugs in your idea. He prefers to play it safe till he's completely sold on your idea—or you.
DUDLEY DENSE	— He rejects anything he doesn't understand. If your idea doesn't make sense to him, he'll tune you out. He'll never be caught buying a pig in a poke. He's not the probing kind, either; he figures it's your idea so it's your job to explain it to his satisfaction.
JEALOUS JOHN	— He's jealous because he didn't think of it first! Not especially creative himself, he feels inferior in the presence of creative thinking people. He's pretty certain if it wasn't his idea, it couldn't be much!
FEARFUL FRED	— You're a threat to him because your idea could endanger his job or his "empire." It

might eliminate his job, mean lost budget dollars, or worse yet, cause him more work. He prefers a comfortable status quo.

PERCY PRESTIGE — Your idea steps on his toes! It implies he hasn't been doing his job as well as he might. It damages his prestige and jeopardizes his real or imagined status.

HESITANT HAROLD — He's terrified of making a mistake and the finality of making a decision worries him. He'll throw up numerous smokescreens and create irrelevant diversions simply to postpone a decision. If he can get your proposal tabled indefinitely, he'll be happy.

BUSY BART — He hasn't time to be bothered with your idea. He has too much unspeculative work to do to lose valuable time exposing his mind to something different. He'll go to great lengths to avoid even listening to your idea, but when finally trapped, keeps his mind preoccupied during the presentation.

INDIFFERENT IKE — Even though it's his responsibility, the problem your idea is trying to solve is not really *his* problem so he can't get too excited about it. Procrastination is his best defense against these ideas which he knows will require effort on his part—but little reward.

MOODY MORTIMER — His immediate health, personal problems, crises, the day's driving conditions, a poor breakfast or lunch, are all more important to him than your idea. He simply can't switch perspectives quickly. On a good day, he'll love your idea, but on a bad day, he'll hate it.

That's your committee; a tough looking lot, isn't it? You may have to sell only one member or a combination of several—or perhaps all of them. You'll find them irritating, stubborn, short-sighted, often ignorant and petty, inconsistent, narrowminded, frequently behind the times—but they're absolutely essential to the successful development of any good idea. They are the devil's advocates who force creative thought at the *presentation* as well as the *inventive* stage, and in spite of themselves will often help you turn half-baked ideas into good, solid ones. Learn to understand these people—their strengths and their weaknesses—and you'll discover how to deal with them. Then you'll be well on your way to convincing them of the merit of your ideas.

TEN WAYS TO SELL YOUR IDEAS

Of course there are nearly as many good techniques for selling ideas as there are ideas to sell, but if you follow these ten basic proven guidelines you'll find you can be successful in selling almost anything to your "committee members."

1. Plan your idea carefully.
2. Explain it carefully.
3. Time it carefully.
4. Use showmanship.
5. Make it believable.
6. Use good judgement.
7. Invite participation.
8. Invite testing.
9. Be innovative.
10. Be persistent.

Take a look at some actual instances where idea people have come into contact with one or more "committee members" and have solved their problems in a dynamic, creative manner.

1. Plan your idea carefully

The first principle of selling anything is to know your product—its capabilities and its weaknesses. The second is to know your customer—his likes and dislikes, his needs, and why he thinks and acts as he does. Without this knowledge, a salesman stands little chance of selling his product. The same is true of an idea. You must understand it well yourself in order to sell it to someone else, and you must understand that "someone else" in order to know how to reach him with your idea.

Think your idea through completely. Prepare it so it will satisfy Dudley Dense and Suspicious Sam. Answer (on paper) the questions, "What is it?" "What will it do?" and "Why is it necessary?" List the negative as well as the positive points of your idea. It will help you anticipate objections and be prepared for them. Be sure to list *all* it will do. Never undersell a good idea. Then plan a strong, dynamic presentation!

> When the veteran ad manager, Suspicious Sam, snapped at his copywriter, "Give me one good reason why this hairbrained campaign of yours should sell more product than the one we're using!", the young man replied, "I'll do better than that—I'll give you two dozen!" and he proceeded to read a list of questions and answers he had prepared regarding his proposal. Impressed by his preparation, the manager bought the idea before the writer reached question-answer #12.

> A major camping equipment manufacturer was in trouble. Sales were down and they were losing their share of the market. One dealer summed up the problem: "You've lost touch with the camper's needs." The president agreed, and ordered his staff into the woods to get the camper's viewpoint once again. They now use camping trips to conceive, develop, and sell new products. Research and Development men take periodic camping trips where they plan new product ideas. Sales and marketing executives take new products along on camping trips to discuss selling campaigns; sales executives invite customers on camping trips to introduce new products to them and to get to know them better.
> They have found this effective in reaching the Busy Barts who seldom have time to listen in the office.

2. Explain It Carefully

Be clear and concise. Talk the other fellow's language. Keep it simple, understandable, and free from jargon and doubletalk. Take each Dudley Dense aside beforehand and explain the idea personally and carefully. Give him a chance to mull it over in his mind before you hit him again with your formal presentation. Reassure Jealous John, Fearful Fred, and Percy Prestige by showing them how your idea will help and even enhance their position rather than endanger it. Clarify things for Suspicious Sam and Hesitant Harold. Explain how your idea affects cost, appearance, safety, operation, use of materials, efficiency, and, of course, profits. Explain in detail how your idea could be put into effect, but leave room for the ideas of others. Be thorough yet brief enough to hold Busy Bart's attention.

As salesman Don Tolliver walked toward the executive offices of a large clothing store, he noticed a sign that read:

The bitterness of poor quality remains long after the sweetness of low price is forgotten

He jotted it down and proceeded to meet the store owner, Suspicious Sam, to sell him a control system. Sam seemed interested until price was quoted. His reply was, "Our present system's a lot less expensive." Don discussed the numerous benefits of his system over the others, but with no success. So he read the owner the words from his own sign. The gentleman chuckled, said "You're giving me a taste of my own medicine," and gave him the order.

A young account executive was making a presentation to Dudley Dense. He closed his summation of the market potential with the statement, "We have scarcely achieved a peripheral penetration in this ambiguous area." His partner, a senior copywriter, noted the puzzled expression on Dense's face and realized the young man had lost him. So he spoke up. "I hate to contradict my partner, but I feel we've just barely scratched the surface of this mixed-up market!" Mr. Dense brightened and said, "That's just what I was thinking!" The presentation proceeded to its successful conclusion.

3. Time It Carefully

Be patient and pick the right time to propose your idea. It often requires careful planning and some cagey psychology, but it will pay off. The time of day, or even the day itself, can mean the difference between success and failure in selling an idea. Try to hit Fearful Fred between traumatic experiences; don't bring up a costly idea during budget-cutting time. Catch Moody Mortimer between blue funks; present your idea when he's in a good mood.

See Jealous John right after he's been successful in selling an idea of his own. Pick the time when your idea is needed most by Hesitant Harold and Indifferent Ike, then tie in dramatically with the needs of the moment. Avoid Fridays when everyone (especially Busy Bart) is tired and rushing to finish the week's work. For the benefit of Suspicious Sam and Dudley Dense, answer questions of timing: Is the idea seasonal? What cycle of time will it be good for? For how long will it benefit the users? Try to make sure that those who must decide on the idea are not rushed and are mentally relaxed and apparently looking for something new to think or talk about. If you see the idea may be premature, let it age before attempting to sell it. But if the time is right, don't allow your idea to be shelved.

An insurance agent watched a prominent banker, Hesistant Harold, pause as he was about to sign an application for a sizable life policy. "On second thought," the banker said, "I think I'd like to give this matter some further consideration. Leave the data with me and come back in a week." The agent replied, "All right, but I wish you would sign this memorandum for me." He handed Harold his business card on the back of which he had written, "I agree to be alive and well one week from today." "I can't sign that!" the banker exclaimed, "How do I know I'll be alive?" "Exactly!" said the agent. The banker grinned sheepishly, took the application, and signed it.

A neophyte artist accompanied his art director to help a presentation of some new ideas to the boss, Moody Mortimer. As they approached the office, the art director suddenly said to the secretary, "Dot, please tell the boss that I've been called out of the building on an emergency and I'll set up another time with him." The girl gave him a knowing wink and agreed. As they retraced their steps, the artist asked, "Why did you do that? We were all ready!" The director replied, "Yes, but the boss wasn't. See the sign by the in-out basket? It's a little barometer I've worked up with her. When the blue side shows, it means the boss has had a good day and is in a receptive mood—the perfect time for showing him ideas. When it's yellow, it's just a so-so day, and ideas *can* be shown to him if they won't wait another day or two. But when it shows red, like it is right now, that means he's in a terrible mood and the likelihood of his changing is zero—about the same chance our ideas would have if we went in there now. We'll try again when the odds are more favorable."

4. Use Showmanship

Make strong use of the visual when making your presentation. Bring all of your creative power tools into play—ENLARGE, MODIFY, COMBINE, etc. Use diagrams, sketches, pictures, flip charts, movies, slides, or working models—all with plenty of color! According to psychologists, when you use words only, listeners will recall 70% of what you say three hours later, and 10% three days later. If you use visual means only, the viewers will recall 85% of your message three hours later, and 65% three days later. This makes people like Suspicious Sam and Dudley Dense feel much more comfortable with your idea.

When you're making your pitch, try the duet or trio approach. A Huntley-Brinkley dialogue will keep interest higher than a straight monologue. Make it good, but keep it in relation to the value of the idea. You don't need a Broadway extravaganza to sell a new model paperclip.

Showmanship is an especially effective method to use in selling ideas to Busy Bart and Indifferent Ike because it entertains as well as instructs.

> Rich Cluchey, a convict and would-be actor, organized a dramatic group among the prisoners and directed dozens of plays put on by the inmates. When Rich was finally paroled, he wanted to push for what he felt were much-needed prison reforms, but he found the "outside world" heavily populated with Indifferent Ikes who cared little one way or the other about the lot of convicts. He decided to make his appeal more dramatic, so he founded Barbwire Theatre, a non-profit organization whose sole purpose is to promote penal reform. The group tours the country, playing to packed houses. It presents a drama written by Rich himself, entitled "The Cage," which portrays the cruelty of many of our present penal practices. After the 80-minute one-act play, the actors (all ex-convicts) come out and partake in a question-answer discussion session with the audience. This creative approach to a sticky social problem has won many strong supporters for reform.

When you're competing with other presentations to get your idea across, you may find it necessary to use a little *extra* showmanship—something which will cause the Busy Barts to remember you and your idea.

> Milton Bellow, an advertising executive, was to make a presentation to a major prospective client. When it came his turn to enter the conference room, he walked in with the rest of his presentation team—but with his hat still on. His colleagues were horrified! When the presentation was over, they chided him and asked why he hadn't removed his hat. He replied, "That client would never have remembered me, what with all the other agency heads he's seeing. Now he'll never be able to forget me!" His agency got the account.

One word of warning: when you use showmanship, make sure you rehearse and plan it carefully. A "blooper" can do irreparable harm to your idea, as in this case:

> A sales manager was presenting the fine points of his distillery's new plastic liquor bottles. In addition to being lightweight, it was also breakproof—and as he said the word "breakproof" he intentionally dropped the bottle on the buyer's floor. True, the bottle didn't break—but it cracked, and a full fifth of bourbon poured all over the floor. The demonstration led to a swift NO SALE!

5. Make It Believable

Be straightforward. Don't oversell or promise more than your idea can deliver. Understatement and conservative estimates do a much better job than rash promises in appealing to intelligent listeners like Suspicious Sam. (They're much easier to live up to, also!) Draw upon the endorsement of prestige figures or those with strong experiences in the area you're discussing. You'll find Hesitant Harold and Busy Bart especially receptive to this technique. If it's good enough for the "experts," it's good enough for them.

> Edward Diedrich, sales manager for a check writing service, was disturbed by a listless sales curve. His inquiries into the problem brought almost identical replies from his salesmen: "There

are too many Hesitant Hanks and Dudley Denses out here: they simply don't see the real need for our service. Our abstract talk about protection against theft and forgery isn't reaching them!"

Ed decided a different presentation was in order, so he contacted the local parole board and asked to be put in touch with an expert but reformed forger. When he found the right man he offered him a sales territory. "I want you," said Ed, "to demonstrate all the tricks of your old trade to these prospective customers. Show them how checks can be removed from conventional sealed envelopes and how easy it is to forge checks. Then show them how our special envelopes and unforgable check machines can prevent this."

The skillful ex-con was so successful that he was able to increase sales nearly 200% in his territory. The pleased sales manager brought him to the home office where he conducted training classes in which the rest of the sales force learned the fine art of forgery. Edward Diedrich now has a complete force of "Honest forgers" in the field—plus a beautifully elevated sales curve.

6. Use Good Judgment

Know *who* you must sell; then aim your message at him or her. Fit the tone of your message to the temperament of your listener. If you're trying to sell Busy Bart, don't attempt to browbeat or ramrod your idea through. Simply be firm and persistent. If you're talking to Fearful Fred or Percy Prestige, make your idea easy to accept by presenting it in a calm, confident manner. Try not to stir up any more controversy than necessary. If you're dealing with Hesitant Harold or Indifferent Ike, and you see you're not going to get the "yes" you were after, take every means possible to avoid getting a flat "no." Recommend a small budget to use in gathering more facts, getting a cost estimate, making a patent search, or (as a last resort) the appointment of a committee to give the idea further study. It's usually easier to resurrect a "maybe" than a "forget it!" Don't be afraid of a soft sell approach. It may seem the long way around sometimes, but it can often get you where you want to go much sooner than any other method. Here's an example:

Because many of its cross-country flights were leaving daily (and unprofitably) from New York only half-booked, a major airline decided a selling job was in order if these flights were to be continued. They hired Stanley Arnold to do the job.

In checking past bookings, Stan determined that the majority of those using cross-country flights were corporation executives, usually at top management level. He attempted some contacts with various presidents but found them to be primarily Busy Barts and Indifferent Ikes who can't be bothered. He discovered that their secretaries nearly always make the reservations, and which airline the executives ride usually depends upon these girls. So he modified his planned approach (remember the MIGHTY MODI-FIER?) and aimed his selling campaign toward the secretaries rather than the executives themselves. The result was a remarkable piece of creative soft sell.

One Monday morning, each of the secretaries of 1,000 corporation presidents in New York City found herself the recipient of a lovely glass bud vase and a single red rose, delivered by special messenger. With each rose was a card which read, "Our airline is thinking of you—we hope you'll think of us the next time the boss needs a cross-country flight." Every Monday morning for a year, these girls received a single red rose and a little personal note from the airline reminding them of the many convenient flights available for the boss's needs.

The plan worked! Cross-country reservations rose more than 60% during that year and many flights were complete sellouts. The airline has continued the rose-a-week program indefinitely.

7. Invite Participation

Create a relaxed, creative atmosphere. Leave time for discussion of your idea. Enlist support for your idea from as many as possible of those who will be involved; do this *before* you make your presentation. Try to have as many of these people as you can present when you show your idea. Be sure to give credit where credit is due concerning the development of your idea. If it wasn't the product of a one-man show, acknowledge it: you'll help sell both your idea and yourself. Sometimes you may find it necessary to arrange for someone else to "have" your idea—like Percy Prestige, the boss, or the most powerful person in the group you're trying to influence. The parentage of an idea oftentimes is not as important as getting the idea put into action.

Invite objections. Anticipate what negative response you're apt to get and be prepared to handle it. Then show both sides of the idea. Leave in a few loopholes which can be easily spotted and easily corrected to give Jealous John a chance to criticize and create on the spot. Once he's contributed to the idea, in even this small way, he's going to be more receptive. After all, it's partly *his* now.

> Clyde Hallowell, company president, decided to make some sweeping reorganizations in his fast-growing firm, but he realized such drastic changes could be accomplished only with the complete cooperation and backing of his top executives and middle management department heads. The latter included several Jealous Johns, Fearful Freds, and Percy Prestiges—all of whom had to be handled with care. So he invited 30 of his key people to a three-day meeting in his sumptuous lakeside lodge in the Colorado mountains, some 500 miles from the home offices.
>
> During the three days, he presented his ideas one at a time, and those present were free to discuss them in a relaxed atmosphere of hospitality rather than hostility. Modifications were made, new ideas suggested by the managers, and problem points discussed and solved by persons who didn't have to worry about rushing to an appointment, commuting, or problems at home. The host-guest atmosphere also helped create much warmer relationships between the president and his people.

8. Invite Testing

Spot the flaws in your idea before Suspicious Sam or Jealous John gets the chance. Before you present it, if possible, test it. Try it out in your own basement or department or territory or classroom. This not only helps you iron out the bugs, it gives you more confidence, plus tangible evidence that it will work. It also provides a basis for estimating costs and a chance to judge initial reactions of others towards your idea. Try to test the market for your idea. If it's too big for you to handle, invite the company to test it. In these days of selective test marketing, you stand a good chance of selling your idea on that basis rather than insisting it go "whole hog" immediately. Testing, even on the smallest scale, can prevent a great deal of embarrassment later on.

> Toby Rogers invented a clever children's game. Before submitting it to a game manufacturer, he tried it out on the children in a fourth grade class where his sister was a teacher. One of

the little girls playing the game sat down and began crying. The teacher asked why and the tearful child pointed to a spot on the game board where she had just landed. It read GO AHEAD THREE SPACES. When she moved the three spaces, she landed on a spot which read GO BACK THREE SPACES. She had been traveling back and forth between the same three spaces for several minutes. Toby modified the board—and ultimately sold the game.

9. Be Innovative

Be prepared to deviate from your prepared plan or approach if the situation demands it. The moment you see you're not getting your idea across to Dudley Dense, or you're losing Busy Bart's attention, or Hesitant Harold starts laying a diversionary smoke-screen, take immediate steps to remedy the situation. This often calls for some quick on-the-spot creative thinking, using power tools like the SUDDEN REVERSALIZER or the SYNTHETIC SUBSTITUTER. Perhaps you'll need a different demonstration, a quick attention-getting action, or you may even have to completely scrap your originally-planned presentation in favor of something specially tailored to the situation at hand.

When Lee Wilkins, a salesman, boasted that his company had everything he might need, his prospective customer Hesitant Harold replied, "I'll bet you don't have any left-handed pencils!" To Lee's questioning, Harold explained the problem of the south-paw whose writing hand moves over what he has written and tends to smudge the written word. Lee thought a moment, smiled, reached into his pocket and pulled out a pencil. "Here is our finest left-handed model—try it and see!" Hesitant Harold did, and was delighted to find his hand didn't smudge the writing. Lee gained a customer and a sizable order. His left-handed pencil? Simply a regulation #3 pencil with hard lead which didn't smudge like the soft-lead pencils Harold had been using.

Once you see you've made your point or your sale, wrap it up —don't continue the presentation. Skip ahead to your closing statement and simply remind the listener that he's made a wise choice in accepting your idea.

Don't limit yourself to a specific formal location for your presentation. If the golf course, a party, or a chance meeting represents a quicker and better opportunity than the office to sell your idea, grab it. Often the informal can be even more effective than the formal pitch.

> Rosser Reeves, an advertising executive, had what he felt was a great idea for promoting a new frozen orange concentrate and wanted to present it to a prospective account. But he couldn't pin down Busy Bart, its president, for an interview. Some months later, the president and his wife were looking for a new home when a real estate broker took them to Rosser's house. They didn't like the house much, but Rosser didn't mind. "What I really wanted to sell you is an ad campaign!" he said, and persuaded the busy president that they could cover the two-hour presentation in just a few minutes. Rosser went to his desk, got a carbon of his pitch, then to his freezer and pulled out several cans of the orange concentrate, and using them as props he made his presentation. He sold the account and the campaign ran for 11 years. It wasn't until much later that Rosser admitted that he'd pre-arranged with the real estate broker to show Busy Bart the house that day!

10. Be Persistent

Have plenty of confidence in your idea yourself. Don't give up too soon; keep plugging away! You can outlast the Hesitant Harolds and Moody Mortimers by simply keeping your cool. If one approach doesn't work, try another; pick a better time; get more data, more presentation material, more help. Don't beat a dead horse, but if your idea is a sound one don't be embarrassed about presenting it a second or third time—or more, if necessary.

If you don't sell your idea at the time, plant seeds for the next presentation. Leave them with something, whether a written summary, a sample, or a memory of something dramatic you said—or did.

> For months, George Arthurson, a retail clerk, tried unsuccessfully to present his idea for a new department to the store manager, Moody Mortimer. "Someday soon, when things calm down a little, I promise. . ." Mortimer would say, but somehow he was always going from one crisis to another. Then from the manager's daughter, who was working as a part-time clerk in the store,

George learned that the high-strung Mortimer's only form of relaxation was the 30-minutes a day he devoted to working complicated jigsaw puzzles. Putting his IDEA RESURRECTOR to work, George came up with an idea. He condensed his presentation to question-answer form and typed it on a large sheet of paper; he had an artist illustrate it with charts, diagrams, and sketches of the finished department as he visualized it. Then he pasted and laminated the paper atop a complicated jigsaw puzzle, broke it apart, and mailed a few pieces of the puzzle each day to Moody Mortimer. At the end of two weeks he mailed the last dozen pieces —minus one—the one on which the cost of the idea was printed. The next day, he received a call from the manager asking him to come to the office to discuss his idea—and to please bring along the missing piece! George sold his idea—and was given the new department to manage.

When you receive a "no," analyze it. It may well be based upon a legitimate problem, which must be solved before you persist in your presentation. Make what modifications are necessary, and try again!

Wylie Jenks, sales manager of a large but relatively green sales force, realized the need for continuous training for his men in the fundamentals of selling and further awareness of the product's capabilities. He was irritated to learn that a written self-help course which he had sent out had been all but neglected. "Just no time to read it!" the men responded. So he tested a course on phonograph records, but with similar results. "When we *are* home, there's no time to play the phonograph!" the men replied. Then Wylie read a statistic that the average salesman spends over 27 hours a week in his car driving from call to call. He contacted a marketing firm which had devised a series of sales improvement lessons which could be played by cassette in a man's car. The men responded to this because they were listening during otherwise "dead" time—not on their valuable leisure time. Sales increased almost immediately as the salesmen gained confidence in their product and new selling skills.

The ability to sell, as we have said, is a vital talent which must become a natural part of your dynamic personality. Don't feel you can leave selling to the "professionals." Selling is something everyone must do, regardless of his or her profession.

The salesman has his product to sell: if he does so in a dynamic, creative manner, he becomes a successful salesman; if not, he's just another man out making calls and filling in expense reports.

The executive or businessman has himself to sell—to his boss, his employees, his customers. If he does a competent, creative job, he will be promoted; if not, he flounders and becomes frustrated and incompetent.

The dynamic person has ideas to sell—to anyone and everyone who might be able to use those ideas. If he presents his ideas creatively, he'll convince others of their worth; if not, he may find himself years later still pondering "What might have been."

Sell your idea. It's the *least* you can do for it!

IDEAS FOR SELLING YOUR IDEAS

Often the hardest part of selling an idea is getting that idea down on paper in a clear, understandable manner. Practice doing this by listing your *three* pet ideas on a sheet of paper, explaining them as completely as you can in a few words. Then list the mental crutches you must discard before you can effectively sell these ideas. Next, list the mental crutches you must convince the "committee" to discard before they will accept your idea.

Now, with these in mind, list at least six good ideas you might use to sell each idea. Before you start, re-read the ten basics listed in the early part of this chapter.

10

How Dynamic Teaching Can Help You Have a More Meaningful Business and Personal Life

> *The principal goal of education is to create men who are capable of doing new things, not simply repeating what generations have done —men who are creative, inventive, and discoverers.*
>
> Jean Piaget

You don't have to be a school teacher to read this chapter. In fact, there are probably tens of millions of "teachers" in this country right at this very moment who have never taken a single college course in education, who don't have a teaching certificate, and who have yet to draw a cent from a board of education or private institution.

If you are a supervisor, a department head, or an executive of any kind—you are a teacher.

If you are a parent—you are a teacher.

If you show a new person the ropes on the job—you are a teacher.

If you are a big brother or sister, aunt or uncle, or a grandparent—you are a teacher.

If you are a writer or an artist—you are a teacher.

If you are an entertainer—you are a teacher.

Anytime you help another human being to take a step forward by learning or doing—*you are a teacher.*

There are good teachers and bad teachers. There are those dynamic teachers and supervisors who spot the creative spark in another human being, nurture it, fan it, and cause it to ultimately burst out in its full power. And there are those who carelessly ignore this creative spark, or, if they do spot it, ruthlessly snuff it out as though it were about to endanger the whole world with its brilliance.

In short, there are those who make teaching others a meaningful, creative act, and those who merely hammer home instructions in a rigid, didactic, pedantic manner. The purpose of this chapter is to demonstrate how you, as a dynamic person, using the creative techniques you've learned thus far, can make whatever teaching you may do more satisfying and effective to you as well as a creative catalyst for those who will learn from you.

First of all, don't let the term "teaching" throw you. It means much more than simple instruction. Dynamic, creative teaching might more appropriately be called "Person Building"—because that's just what it can and should do. A Memphis school teacher once summed up the mission and the requirements of all dynamic teachers this way:

> The teacher's whole soul must be bent on making her students come alive. She must be a master salesman—and competition is keen. In order to prod the lazy, to lure the difficult, to encourage the slow, and to guide them all, she must possess the charm of a Cleopatra, the wiles of a Machiavelli, the patience of Job, the gentleness of St. Francis, the wisdom of Solomon—and the imagination of Disney!

One of your obligations as a dynamic person is to be a dynamic teacher—to communicate ideas and ideals to *your children* and *those who influence your children*, and in turn help them formulate and communicate their own ideas and ideals. The kind of world your youngsters and their youngsters will someday live in depends a great deal upon their ability to generate ideas to cope with an increasingly complicated environment. Much of this ability they will owe to you!

WHEN YOU TEACH, BE IMAGINATIVE!

In teaching your children, you must realize that the so-called generation gap could more aptly be described as an "idea gap." That which you have to communicate to your youngsters is just as valid and important as it was five, ten, or two dozen years ago—but you must remember that you're not communicating it five, ten, or two dozen years ago. You're dealing with today! And today's learners have seen everything! They've been exposed to literally thousands of tricks of attention-getting, entertainment, and teaching through TV, colorful children's books and magazines, phonograph records, toys, and even their cereal boxes. They see and listen to polished, highly-paid professionals right in their living rooms every day. In fact, the average child during the first 18 years of his life will have been exposed to between 15,000 and 20,000 hours of television viewing! The Captain Kangaroos and the Walt Disneys make learning interesting and fun. They stimulate young minds.

If you attempt to reach these same youngsters in the severe, monotonous fashion once employed (perhaps on you) by Miss Picklewick of Public School 110, you'll lose them—and fast! Not because your message isn't important, but because you didn't make it *seem* important. Present your message imaginatively and enthusiastically and you can compete with the TV "pros." Present it in a dull, routine manner and you may not even be competing with the weather reports.

If yours is the job of teaching *your employees* or *co-workers*, you have another important obligation—to give them your creative best. A person's whole attitude toward his job and the company he works for can be formed during the first few weeks or months of his employment.

LEARN THE PRINCIPLES OF DYNAMIC TEACHING

In these next few pages we will explore the principles of DYNAMIC TEACHING. Many of the case histories we've used are those of school teachers, and this is intentional because *they* are the *pros* in this business of person building. Obviously, though, it takes more than school teachers alone to build responsible, creative people. It takes supervisors, executives, parents, religious leaders, friends, public servants, entertainers—creative people in all walks of life. Let's begin our exploration by listing the basics of DYNAMIC TEACHING:

D . . . **Dedication.** Be sincerely interested in teaching and genuinely enthusiastic about whatever you're teaching. Stimulate those you're teaching; make the subject something they *want* to learn about. Encourage dedication in others who have the task of teaching. Give them the desire and the wherewithal to do their best.

Y . . . **"You" power.** Humanize your approach by being a real person to those you're teaching, not just a symbol of authority. Use every facet of your dynamic personality to communicate your interest, concern, and love to them —and do it often!

N . . . **"New" power.** Introduce them to the stimulation and excitement that comes from doing or learning something new and different, then *keep* them exposed to variety and away from deadly ruts. Use the *new* yourself—new techniques, new methods, new devices. You can teach "new" by using the "new."

A . . . **Adaptation.** Draw upon today's available tools; adjust your methods to the needs and environment of those you're teaching. Transpose! Good ideas are available from every conceivable field today: business, retailing, advertising, entertainment, politics, science—everywhere. Take advantage of all this creative effort by adapting it to your particular needs and situation.

M . . . **Modification.** Be flexible! If the old format no longer does the job, try a different one or revise the present procedure to make it less severe or uncompromising. Be quick to substitute or rearrange. Nothing stays the same for long; why should your lesson plans, classroom, home or office be any exception?

I . . . **Intellectual stimulation.** Expose your "learners" to the sensuous pleasure of using their minds constantly and creatively. Challenge them to think, then help them toward the satisfaction that comes from acting on their thoughts.

C . . . **Creativity.** Use it yourself, and stimulate it in others.

Replace rote with curiosity, oppression with expression, and open the mental toolshed and expose them to the multitude of available creative tools. Be a creative instructor and you'll have creative learners.

Those are the principles, now let's put them into practice!

BE DEDICATED

Dedication begins at home—with you, the parent. Sure, you have a right to expect your children's teachers to be dedicated, but its even more important to begin at the beginning in this vital area. You must be a dedicated parent, too!

The pre-school or kindergarten teacher is no less a teacher than one who handles first, fifth, or tenth grade; hers is the job to prepare youngsters for the coming schooling they will receive. In the same way, you, as a dynamic parent, are a teacher with the awesome role of preparing the minds of your children for the education they are to receive. Your role as a parent should be to encourage creative, original thought and action in your youngsters. As you do this, keep in mind these things:

Everything he does, need *not* be useful.
Everything he does, need *not* be successful.
Everything he does, need *not* be perfect.
It isn't necessary that everyone he knows likes him.
Solitude can be as important as togetherness.

Children need solitude and independence for thinking and dreaming, and even imperfect or unsuccessful creative efforts should be encouraged because individual thinkers may have to go against accepted ideas or norms. Do what you can to encourage a creative atmosphere. Allow your children to be individuals whether at home, at school, or at play. Be sure they are aware of the creative tools available, then help and encourage them to use these tools. If your children's home or school atmosphere stifles rather than promotes creativity, change it—and the sooner the better!

Mr. and Mrs. Ulrich were attending family night at the local primary school. In the room where one of their children was enrolled, they were amazed to see the walls circled by drawings of

45 Thanksgiving turkeys. Each was signed to indicate who drew it, but otherwise all turkeys were identical—the same size, color and number of feathers. The teacher proudly labeled it "artistic discipline" when the parents questioned her about the "carbon copies" of her original design. In the next room, the teacher boasted about her ability to keep 45 youngsters absolutely still and quiet for the 50-minute periods when they were in her class. No questions, no discussions—just silence. In commenting on the two incidents to the principal, Mr. and Mrs. Ulrich were dismayed to learn that he considered these teachers "examples" for the rest of his faculty. Within two months, the family moved to another school district—one in which creativity was encouraged rather than killed at an early age.

A *dedicated parent* can and should promote dedication in teachers, too. Besides the obvious, such as encouraging qualified, dynamic people to enter the teaching profession and seeing that they have the money and facilities to do their jobs well, it's important to give them adequate support in other ways. They need the stimulation of knowing parents are behind them and appreciate their dedication and skill. Here's how one thoughtful parent accomplished this:

Two school teachers attending a convention in a New York hotel were pleasantly surprised when a waiter informed them that someone had picked up the check for their meal. They thought there had been some mistake until the waiter showed them a note another customer had given him along with the payment. It read:

Don't take any money from these teachers. I have two boys in school. I owe so much to the teachers. Thanks.

During the convention business meeting, the incident was mentioned—and it brought the loudest and longest applause of the day.

To sustain one's dedication sometimes requires some positive, creative thinking. Even the most dedicated teacher, professional or otherwise, is going to have moments of depression and will find himself wondering, "Is it really worth it?" These are moments for which the dynamic person must be prepared—as is this veteran teacher:

Ted Gallin keeps a folder into which he places notes and letters he receives from time to time from parents, principals, and pupils complimenting or thanking him. When the going gets rough and discouragement threatens, he takes out the letters and "recharges his batteries" by reading them through.

See how important it can be to "keep those cards and letters coming, folks!" When your child is fortunate enough to get a dynamic, creative teacher, take a few minutes from time to time to pay that teacher a compliment. Remember Mark Twain's remark, "I can go for a whole week on one compliment," and show your appreciation—often!

A *dedicated supervisor* is a stimulating teacher, too. He is sincerely interested in the end result of his efforts and often goes to great lengths to make the learning process of his employees both interesting and long lasting. He looks beyond the immediate. He is able to envision the dynamic, creative individual of tomorow he is helping to develop today.

Stimulating people to learn is a task that calls for imagination and a wealth of ideas. Here's an example from the world of sales:

Hank Tindle, a divisional sales manager for a large corporation, takes a personal hand in training all his new salesmen. After several weeks of routine training, each neophyte spends a week making the rounds with Hank. It is a traumatic experience which leaves an indelible impression on the new men. In the course of making his calls during that week, Hank runs into every conceivable type of tough customer, from the yelling, screaming "Get out and stay out" type to the quiet, uncommunicative type. He handles each in a smooth, professional manner, and ends up with a sale and an appointment for a return visit. What the neophyte doesn't know (until his week is ended) is that each customer has, in advance, agreed to play a "role" for Hank whenever he enters their store with a new man. The "script" is prearranged, the outcome certain, and the results very effective. The new man learns firsthand some very important rules of salesmanship, and Hank further cements relations with key customers—who are flattered that he sought their help.

COMMUNICATE ON A ME-TO-YOU BASIS!

"You" power is worth a hundred books, or more! There's no substitute for personal contact between the "teacher" and the taught—especially when the teacher is a dynamic, creative and interested person. Make your teaching a form of personal me-to-you communication. Don't confuse "teaching" with "preaching," which is what many people (especially businessmen) do when they attempt to put across a message. Employers, for example, often tend to rely on bulletins, house magazines, plant broadcasts, and the like, to convey new programs or policies. These are frequently received by employees in much the same way a student receives a boring lecture—with apathy. When you personalize your message, you make it far more effective. Here's an example of "you-power" in action:

A management consultant firm making an employee-attitude survey for a large midwest utility was surprised to find how popular with employees was a monthly column written by the President, James Olcott, for the company magazine. They not only read it avidly and thoroughly but also remembered a great deal of what they had read. Employees would quote directly from editorials and cite facts and figures mentioned in them. Further interviewing by the consultants uncovered why. One of Mr. Olcott's first acts upon taking office was to go through every office and throughout the plant, meeting and shaking hands with every single one of the thousands of persons on the company payroll. It was a tremendous undertaking, but he completed it, establishing a unique rapport with his employees. As one plant supervisor put it, "I know Mr. Olcott personally. I've talked with him. When I read his editorials, it's just like he and I are sitting here together and he's telling me how things stand. He tells me the things I like to know—the bad as well as the good!"

"You power" means *your* power as a parent, too. Teaching isn't something you as a parent can afford to leave to the "professionals." It has to start right from birth. Your youngsters don't suddenly turn on their "learning equipment" when they enter grade school. They've had it all along, but whether you've kept it in good repair depends on you, as parents. You can begin building a dynamic, creative personality in your child right from the very beginning by using close personal contact and creative teaching methods. The importance—and effectiveness—of this is seen in these impressive results from a study conducted recently by the National Institute of Mental Health:

> Of a group of 64 15-month old babies from low income, poorly educated families, half were given an hour's tutoring a day by women college graduates acting as "part-time mothers" who read, talked and played with them. At age three, the tutored and untutored children were tested. The babies who had had the "part-time mothers" scored an average IQ of 106, compared with 89 for the untutored group. In its published report, the Institute issued this warning: "Regardless of economic status, maternal neglect seems to retard children's development . . . conversely, thoughtful, loving attention can help children reach their intellectual potential."

You needn't restrict your parental teaching to books, educational toys, trips to the zoos, and the like. An appropriate, well-timed object lesson or moral tied to an everyday happening can be a good, creative learning device. Here's a heart-warming example:

> A father watched his young son struggle vainly to lift a heavy box. Finally he asked the youngster, "Are you using *all* your strength?" "Sure I am!" replied the exasperated boy. "No you're not," the father said, "you haven't asked *me* for help yet."

TRY NEW METHODS, NEW IDEAS!

"New power" is, in many ways, as vital as "you power," because unless the human mind is constantly stimulated by the new—new sights, new sounds, new tastes, new experiences, new words, new ideas, new skills, new dreams, new horizons—it begins tuning out instead of tuning in. This isn't restricted to the young mind, either; it happens to adults, too.

Dynamic teaching requires experimentation, versatility, and the ability to keep up with the times. The fact that something was interesting in your day is not a guarantee that it will stimulate today's youngsters. Be ready and willing to try something new!

An exasperated Betty Crane was angry with her senior English class. The students were merely "putting in time" and doing the minimum necessary to pass and graduate. Using a SYNTHETIC SUBSTITUTER approach, she decided to try a different type of term project: to write, direct, produce and film a 30-minute color melodrama on a western theme. The students did research papers on whichever aspect of the operation they wanted to handle, such as camera, lighting, makeup and producing. The paperwork was evaluated for its grammar and composition, thus showing the students the practical application of those skills. Class members selected ideas for the script from their original short stories, then they divided up for group discussions according to their interests. Those concerned with camera collaborated with the director in the shooting of each scene; those interested in music worked together to choose appropriate themes for the action on the screen. The movie took nearly six months to make, using two class hours a week, plus evening and early morning hours. Total cost, including color film, was under 20 dollars. Results: the most enthusiastic group of seniors to graduate in years!

"New power" works on "older" people, too. The old rules of "Do it and don't argue" may have enforced a certain efficiency among employees once upon a time, but it did little to turn out creative, dynamic workers. Your people will respond to education —but not to intimidation. When you feel the necessity to "force" interest in your employees, do so using positive rather than negative methods. This can and should stimulate your people's creative efforts rather than squelch them. Here's how one dynamic manager used a new approach to educate his workers:

Thorne Franklin, manager of a large retail store, felt his buyers were too set in their ways. Their purchases often lacked imagination and their methods hadn't changed in recent years. So he started a series of classes in "Modern Retailing Methods" to be attended by his entire staff of buyers every Monday morning. Once a month, he would conduct the classes himself. The other times he had different buyers explain how their departments operated, their buying philosophy, tricks of the trade which they used, and recent ideas which they had put into play resulting in more sales. The classes worked well. Buyers began picking up ideas from unrelated departments and adapting them to their own; they became more enthusiastic as competition developed to see who would win the "Buyer of the Week" award—a plaque (and cash prize) presented to the one who had done the most creative and successful job of merchandising. At the end of six months, total store sales had increased nearly 20%, with some departments showing increases as high as 300%!

You may, at times, discover, that "something new" is really something old or temporarily forgotten, but still basically sound. Take the case of these two dynamic "teachers" from the retail world:

> Foster Nye and his wife, owners of a small store in a suburban neighborhood, were plagued with juvenile shoplifters, but in the interest of customer relations did little about it. Finally, however, the losses became too great to ignore, so the couple devised a plan. Whenever they caught a young person in the act of stealing, they called the parents and asked them to come to the store. They informed the family that, rather than turning the child over to the police, they would give him the opportunity of working for the store until he had earned enough to pay for the item he had taken. Then he was allowed to keep it. The plan worked well. Most parents agreed, and to their surprise discovered the youngsters found great stimulation in a new adventure—called "work." Many became "permanent part-time" employees of the store afterwards, and the owners were pleased to find pilfering had dropped to almost nothing.

CROSS-POLLINATE—ADAPT IDEAS FROM ELSEWHERE

Adaptation (remember the ALL-PURPOSE ADAPTER from your creative storehouse?) is a powerful tool just waiting for your use as a dynamic teacher. There are probably more usable ideas floating around now than during any other ten generations in history. TV, movies, the business world, science—all offer hundreds of thousands of new ideas which you can adapt to the job of educating people. Cross-pollinate: borrow, swipe, transpose, from these everyday ideas and use them in your particular situation in the home, office, store or classroom. Adapt from the entertainment industry. Use movies, TV, and film strips to train the new people at work. Better still, let them create their own, as in this instance:

The board of directors for the Worldwide Corporation decided they wanted a short color movie on the company and how it operates, for presenting to the stockholders at the next annual meeting. They gave the task to Norm Patman. At first Norm resented the assignment because he had a group of three new employees he was trying to train. Then he decided to accomplish both jobs at once. He turned the task of researching, writing and preparing the film over to the new people, and made himself available only as an advisor as needed. The people responded well, and with the aid of a professional cameraman, turned out an outstanding film. When they finished, they were not only well-grounded in the total operation—they had become enthusiastic "company men" as well.

Adapt devices from the business world when you're teaching young people. Retailers, for example, use some highly creative devices to interest people in stores and products. Transpose some of these devices for use in your own particular situation. Here's a classroom example:

Algebra isn't the most stimulating subject for ninth graders, George Fogel, their teacher, discovered, so he began searching for ways to make it more interesting. Noticing the effectiveness with which local stores were using trading stamps as extra incentive, he decided to try a similar approach in his classroom. He mimeographed sheets of stamps which he called flash stamps (Flash being a nickname given him by his students). The stamps were given for extra work done by the pupils—things such as voluntarily turning in brain-teasers, doing extra problems, giving reports, or other special projects. The stamps are redeemable. In place of a missing assignment, he will accept ten flash stamps; the student may use his stamps to get out of detention—the choices are numerous. He has found that many students never redeem the stamps; they simply collect them to see who has the most at the end of the year.

Diversification works in the business world; why shouldn't you promote its use in the field of education, too? It can be effective in many different ways, as evidenced by this incident:

Why should a library confine itself to lending only books, Hazel Rigby, a high-school librarian, asked herself, and she decided to see what response her students would make if the library were to loan out cameras and camera accessories. After all, she reasoned, photography can offer young people a highly creative means of self-expression. The school administration agreed and bought her idea.

The library began offering cameras, light meters, film and flash accessories, and loaned them out just like books. Hazel had several real camera bugs available at first to show the beginners how to work the equipment. Initially, the students spent most of the film on crazy photographs of each other, but by their second or third rolls they began trying to capture the world around them like the "pros." Many of the youngsters achieved good results and nearly all became more perceptive.

The school now has an active camera club, a darkroom which the students can use, and classes in photography during the summer sessions.

BE PREPARED TO USE "CHANGE" AS A TOOL!

Modification (the MIGHTY MODIFIER) is a "must" if you're to be a dynamic teacher! *Change* is the keyword for this third of the Twentieth Century, and as a creative person you must be able to acknowledge, act upon, and anticipate change. Good ideas will soon be superseded by better ideas and those, too, will give way someday to even better ones. Stay flexible and be ready and willing to change your approach to teaching your co-workers, or your youngsters should you see that the "same old approach" no longer produces results. See what happened when this agency modified its training methods:

Arnold Ericson, dynamic head of a public-relations advertising agency, had a new account—a national airline. The airline was anxious to project a new image of friendliness and efficiency through its advertising, pilots, stewardesses, and ground personnel. After having his team of copywriters do the usual research on the new client, he asked for ideas. They ranged from average to uninspired. So Arnold decided to modify his training methods. He asked for and received permission for two of his woman writers to take the airline's complete stewardess training course. They did, and as a result not only learned the airline inside and out, but came back to the agency with an exciting supply of ideas and suggestions for future campaigns.

Modify your technique. Give it a new name, a new color, a new atmosphere; make it longer or shorter (many schools, for example, are trying the mini-semester—a complete course given on a crash basis during the two-week mid-semester "holiday"); open it to more people or fewer or those of the opposite sex; if one instructor is not enough, use two or more to handle the subject; don't marry yourself to any single approach. Even the smallest modification can often bring results. Look:

> What's in a name? Arthur Banks, principal of an Ohio high school, was disturbed by the treatment given substitute teachers by the students who often considered the "temporary" as fair game for every kind of disciplinary breach. He brainstormed the problem with his staff, and someone suggested that the word "substitute" itself might be part of the problem since "substitute" is normally associated with something inferior. Mr. Banks agreed, and decreed that the term be dropped and replaced with that of "guest teacher" since "guest" implies treatment of someone in the very best fashion. The reaction was good; students, staff, and the "guest teachers" themselves began reflecting more respect to the person taking over when a teacher is absent.

What could *you* accomplish by changing a few titles at work? By giving your fellow-workers some dynamic nicknames?

STIMULATE THOSE YOU TEACH

Intellectual stimulation is more than a prime goal of teaching; it's also one of its greatest rewards! It is extremely important that you communicate the love and thrill of learning to your youngsters and re-kindle it in adults. When you transmit the feeling of excitement that comes from intellectual enlightenment or accomplishments to another human mind, you have done something that approximates teaching caveman how to light his first fire. You've really started something! It's not always easy. There is plenty of non-intellectual and anti-intellectual competition for the minds of young and old alike today. You'll find you may need all the dedication, you-power, and new-power you can muster. It may even tax your facilities of adaptation and modification to the utmost. But the end result is worth it because you will have enriched yourself intellectually, as well as those you're stimulating. Here's a case from a dynamic home:

Disturbed by the fact that his young children were doing more TV watching than reading, James Kincaid challenged them to compete against him in a book-reading contest. An avid reader himself, he promised the youngsters 10¢ a book for each one they read above the number he himself read each month. The children became regular bibliophiles. At the end of the first year, his ten-year-old daughter had read 278 books, his eight-year-old son 136—both easily topping his own 48! The contest ran from grade-school days through early high school.

Neither age nor position is a guarantee against apathy, and you'll often see adults who appear to have placed a DO NOT DISTURB sign on the door of their mind marked "Intellectual Enrichment." This is as unfortunate as placing a NO IDEAS WANTED notice on your office door, and so it becomes *your* job, frequently, to stimulate not only your young people but also some very adult adults. You can accomplish this using the same principles of creative thought which you use on your youngsters, but perhaps you'll need to embellish them with some ADULTS ONLY stimulators. Here's an executive who did just that:

Joe Zigler, corporation president, found his executives so wrapped up in details of their respective jobs that they were doing little or no reading about new schools of thought, marketing concepts in other fields, and the like. So each time he read what he considered a valuable book he would call his executives together and discuss several points from the book which he felt might relate to their functions. He then offered to loan his copy to anyone interested in reading the book in full. Anxious to impress the boss, the men borrowed or bought copies and read them. He then made it a point to discuss portions of the books with the executives either over lunch or in smaller meetings. For many of these men, this was their first book-reading in years, but once they got started, it was they who began recommending new books—and ideas—to the boss.

Responsibility stimulates interest, and the more responsibility you can give your youngsters or your employees, the more interested and responsive you're going to find them. Never try to force "learning for the sake of learning" on people of any age. Give them a *reason* for learning: relate the results to their future, their growth, or even their immediate job and you'll find your "lesson" much better received. Observe how this creative college professor handled such a situation:

> Professor of Education, Henry Sadelle, didn't need the yawns of his students to tell him that educational films can frequently be boring. He decided, however, rather than to scrap the film program, to take a different tack. He passes out a rating and discussion sheet to all those in his classes as they are about to view such a film. The sheets concern matters such as presentation, effective or ineffective demonstrations, what was considered the best and worst part of the film, what wasn't clear, techniques, direction, and what could have been improved. The pupils must rate the films from excellent to poor. Professor Sadelle has found that being asked to justify their ratings makes students watch films much more attentively. After each viewing, he sends the rating sheets to the producers of the film for their consideration when making future productions.

Don't allow people's energy to dissipate into nothingness! When you find they are anxious to air their opinions, ideas, complaints, or just their vocal cords, be quick to provide them with a creative outlet for their expressions. If you wait till next month or next semester or next year, you many never be able to re-create the enthusiasm of the moment either in yourself or in others.

BUILD CREATIVITY IN YOURSELF— SO YOU CAN BUILD IT IN OTHERS

Creativity, the backbone of a dynamic personality, is also the backbone of a dynamic teacher. Not only must you be creative yourself to communicate your ideas, you must, in turn, help those you to teach to create their own ideas.

Whether you're teaching in the business world, in the home, or at school, it's vital that you maintain an open, creative atmosphere—one free from rote and rigidity, arbitrary do's and don'ts, and other mental crutches which encourage conformity rather than creativity.

Start with your own children: provide them with a creative home atmosphere and encourage their individual development.

> In his college course on Creative Problem Solving, one dynamic teacher warns his married pupils of the "evils" of coloring books for youngsters. He feels that "by starting kids out at such an early age to conform to lines and pictures drawn by other persons, you're shutting off self-expression almost before it begins!" He recommends instead, giving children plenty of pencils and crayons and blank paper and allowing them to scribble whatever comes to mind. Children become more excited about their original creations than they could ever be about "staying in the lines"—the object of formal coloring books. Parents following his advice report good results, not only in their children's increased expression of hidden talents, but also in their enthusiasm for creating.

Curiosity is a strong factor in creativity; stimulate it! Ideas seldom hatch in mental iceboxes filled with nothing but cold, hard facts. Ideas must come from exploration, examination, and experimentation. Give your young people the opportunity to explore and they'll discover combinations and ideas your adult world has never even dreamed of.

It's never too early to start building your people's curiosity into a strong habit. Look at the results in this classroom incident:

> Jumping to conclusions is a habit of many young people which infuriates Lillian Fleisher, a dynamic third-grade teacher. So she keeps a cardboard box with a door cut in front on a table in her classroom, and each Monday she places an object in the box. Throughout the week each student has a chance to reach in and feel the object. The pupil then writes a description of what he has felt. At the end of the week, the children read the descriptions aloud and take the article from the box to examine and discuss it. Initially, the objects are easy to recognize—a toy chair or china dog—but as the weeks progress, the objects become harder to identify—glass eyes from a broken doll's head, for example. Even though they can't identify the object, the students must make their description as specific as they can. They soon learn the danger of jumping to conclusions without careful, thorough exploration. Their reports progress from the very simple to the detailed and their insights and descriptive skills broaden as they write, and listening to their reports read aloud increases their awareness of the need to write clearly and understandably.

How many ways can you stimulate creativity in your new employees or co-workers? Start to work on the problem right away!

DYNAMIC TEACHING IS *YOUR* RESPONSIBILITY

Dynamic teaching, in summary, consists of many things, all of which are vital components of your dynamic personality. Let's review them:

D-edication
Y-ou-power
N-ew-power
A-daptation
M-odification
I-ntellectual stimulation
C-reativity

Dynamic teaching is the job of all adults, from parents to businessmen to teachers, from amateurs to professionals, from the altruistic to those with a specific monetary goal. It can be the most rewarding of tasks or the most frustrating—or both at the same time.

Dynamic teaching is no eight to five job. There are no contracts to protect you against the hours of mental overtime you'll put into it; no tenure to offer you security; and no salary invented that can adequately cover its worth. Yet it is completely rewarding, because teaching another human being is one of the most creative of all human functions. No matter what your vocation, dynamic teaching is *your* lifetime responsibility.

Remember the creative power tools from Chapter 5? Bring them into play again to help you become a more dynamic teacher. On a sheet of paper, list six ways in which you can apply each of these tools to your particular teaching assignment, whether parent, teacher, supervisor, etc.: the ENORMOUS ENLARGER (example: 1. Make the learning period longer, etc.), the COMPACT REDUCER (example: 1. Reduce the size of the class; etc.), the MIGHTY MODIFIER, the REMOVABLE RE-ARRANGER, the SYNTHETIC SUBSTITUTER, the SUDDEN REVERSALIZER, the PERFECT COMBINER, the ALL-PURPOSE ADAPTER, the IDEA RESURRECTOR, and the SYSTEMATIC SEARCHER.

11

How to Develop a More Dynamic Marital and Personal Life

The full answer to the problems of existence lies in true and mature love.

Erich Fromm

Once you've developed your dynamic personality you won't be satisfied with anything less than dynamic, creative performance in every segment of your daily life. It's time, now, to put your efforts to work developing a more dynamic marital or personal life. Your effectiveness in any undertaking is dependent upon your physical and emotional well-being, and if you're having trouble in your marriage, you can't perform at your peak of efficiency on the job or anywhere else.

Let's look, then, at the keys that can unlock your creative powers for complete, effective use in your relationships with the opposite sex. Such a relationship requires, at the very least, the kind of dynamic, creative thinking you give your job, your social activities, or anything else you do. Often it requires more. Most people, however, seldom give this kind of attention to this part of their lives—and this is unfortunate for both parties. In fact, if we fell into the kind of rut in our business activities that we often do with our lifetime partner, many of us would remain on the bottom rung of the success ladder for life!

BE A TOTALLY DYNAMIC PERSON!

A dynamic personality, as we've said before, means being a *totally* dynamic person. It means using your creative energies in every single facet of your life, from solving problems to generating new ideas. One of the purposes of this chapter is to discuss and demonstrate ways in which you can put your creative powers to work building a more fulfilling sex life for you *and* your partner.

Now, a dynamic sex life doesn't mean a 365-day-a-year orgy. Unquestionably, frequent and passionate sexual activity can be good and desirable, and it can do wonders for a marriage relationship. But it can't—and won't—last forever. You should strive for a complete 24-hour-a-day relationship with your partner—a *sensuous* relationship instead of one which is merely *sensual.*

What's the difference? (The two words look and sound so much alike they are frequently misused interchangeably.)

The word *sensual* means appealing to the physical or bodily senses. The sensual side of a sexual relationship is delightful—few people would quarrel with that—and there are many interesting and creative ways to heighten the pleasure of the relationship through the five basic senses.

Touch—A reassuring touch, holding hands, a kiss, an embrace, a caress, sexual activity—all are excellent ways of communicating our feelings.

Taste—Good food and drink can be an effective stimulation to romance.

Smell—A good clean scent, an enticing perfume or after shave are all useful "starters" for turning on your lover.

Sound—Your voice saying the right things at the right time; mood music and favorite tunes; laughter—or sometimes even more valuable, silence; all are "musts" to any relationship.

Sight—Attractive clothes, provocative clothes, or no clothes at all; eye-to-eye contact; long, meaningful looks; beauty marks or tattoos; smiles; beautiful objects such as jewelry, flowers, or presents. They provide a variety of pleasures.

In a purely sensual relationship, then, you will satisfy the bodily appetites, but to stop there is like building a house and leaving off the roof simply because the day is warm and sunny and enjoyable. It doesn't allow for "tomorrow." A totally satisfying, long-term relationship must be *sensuous*—filled with the physical satisfaction of the sensual, but heightened, protected, and lengthened by continuous stimulation of five basic intellectual senses.

Curiosity—Expose your mate and yourself to the new and unusual; surprise her; explore and learn together; put variety in your relationship—it's an effective stimulant!

Excitement—Involve your partner in the thrill of adventure, contest, challenge, drama—anything new and different. The resulting physical and emotional thrill can carry over into a more exciting everyday relationship.

Emotional Concern—Express your feelings of thoughtfulness, respect, consideration, understanding and honesty, and you'll elicit the same from your mate.

Communication—Keep your lines open and use them frequently to express your feelings of love, pride, joy and (when necessary) hate and fear. Sharing your thoughts with one another is important!

Creativity—Everyone has a basic desire to create something— whether it's life, beauty, wisdom, structures, or anything that will survive the here and now. Fulfilling that desire together creates a beautiful relationship as well.

These are the basic senses. In our earlier chapters we have listed and discussed the basic tools available to you in building dynamic, creative ideas and relationships. Where, then, do you begin in relating all this to your sex life?

In a relationship with a person of the opposite sex, you needn't start with "once upon a time." Usually lovers have very few problems in getting started on their relationship; chemistry takes care of most initial hesitations, awkwardness and embarrassment. It's the "happy ever after" that needs working on, because the post-courtship days (and years) are the ones filled with problems— problems that need creative solutions.

As you recall from Chapter 2, the first step in dealing with any problem is to recognize it as a problem, then determine that you are definitely going to deal with it. So let's use that as our starting point. List your problem—or problems—right now. What's keeping your relationship from being all you want? Here are some of the most frequently aired problems:

> "Our marriage is dull and uninteresting—and so is my spouse!"
> "We hardly communicate at all—we're practically strangers!"
> "We just don't have time for anything anymore!"
> "He's selfish and inconsiderate—about sex and everything else!"
> "The only time he/she makes love is when he/she's had something to drink!"
> "He's thoughtless and doesn't care!"
> "He never says he loves me!"
> "All we do is argue!"
> "He's/she's become a real slob—hard even to be around!"
> "We have nothing in common anymore!"
> "Our sex life has become more a chore than a pleasure!"

There are more, of course—perhaps as many more as there are marriages. But let's use these as starters and observe how the techniques of dynamic creative thinking can put new life into ailing relationships.

"Our marriage is dull and uninteresting—and so is my spouse!"

The problem. Chateaubriand pinpointed it in 1802 when he said, "The soul of man becomes weary and never loves the same object long and fully." Nearly 19 centuries earlier a Roman philosopher said, "No pleasure lasts long unless there is variety in it."

To stay meaningful, love must be a constantly growing, developing, maturing thing. If your relationship with your partner hasn't changed much in the past few years, it could be in trouble—and in need of some fresh, new thinking on the part of both of you! You need some variety to spice up your lives. Current best-sellers to the contrary, though, variety doesn't mean changing partners, wife-swapping, group orgies, and the like. This is not only dangerous; it's unnecessary! The dynamic person has the ability and the resources to put enough variety and excitement into a relationship so that it seems constantly new, no matter how old it may be.

What to do. Put the excitement of courtship back into your marriage! Use your creative SYSTEMATIC SEARCHER to help you seek excitement. Don't let routine, no matter how practical or comfortable it may be, dominate your life. Explore life together, the way you did when you were younger. Put new variety into your sensual relationship; be willing to experiment, to "try anything once"! Try new techniques, times, places. Expand your list of sensuous pleasures, too. Discover new interests, go new places, look at new objects, be willing to make a few mistakes and to accept an occasional unpleasant experience. Not only is it stimulating and fun, it also provides you with some fine conversation later on. Have your adventures now; don't stay satisfied all your life with the old ones. Don't list reasons you can't—list ways you *can*—and keep listing them till you do!

Some ideas. A college professor in Creative Problem Solving challenged his students to make their marriages more stimulating by "doing something different." Their brainstorms and subsequent follow-through resulted in ideas like these:

Go back to nature: take walks together, on the beach, through the woods or just around the block; pick berries or wildflowers; go hiking or bikeriding; go swimming at night; make love on the grass.

Try some new entertainment: a "dive" instead of a movie; a museum instead of the Sunday drive; a soccer game instead of TV football; take a boat ride, go horseback riding, jog together; instead of going to PTA, stay home and make love; work a jigsaw puzzle together instead of watching TV.

Change eating habits: try new restaurants—a different one each time you go out; shop in an ethnic grocery store and buy some new food to try.

Prospect new areas of common interest: try art, music, sports, shopping, collecting, social service, literature, redecorating, discussion groups, politics—anything you can both enjoy.

Make new friendships: meet new people; let them introduce you to new places, ideas and other people. Pick them because they're interesting and stimulating, not because they're necessary to job security or social advancement.

We hardly communicate at all—we're practically strangers!

Problem. A serious case of marital complacency. Whenever there's "just nothing to talk about" and the primary conversation becomes "Pass the salt," "While you're up, switch to Channel 5," or "What's the weather out?" a marriage needs some creative help —and fast! Any communication problem should be solved as quickly as possible before the "silent curtain" becomes a sound-proof wall.

What to do. Back up! Think back to when you first met. There was no communication problem then. You had a feeling for your partner which you wanted to convey, and you expressed it, either verbally or physically. Assuming your partner hasn't developed some unusual sense of ESP since that time, you must still express your feelings. In fact, the chances are that your partner needs *more* reassurance of your love now than back then.

> Following a minor accident with her car, Shirley Durham was searching through her husband's financial drawer for the insurance policy. She noticed his last will and testament and out of curiosity, opened it. Inside was an envelope addressed to her. The temptation was too much, so she opened and read it. It was a letter her husband had written intending it to be opened after his death. In it he thanked her for the good life they had shared together and expressed in intimate terms his love for her. That evening she confronted him with the letter and demanded, "Did you mean what you said in here?" "Of course!" he replied. "Then why were you going to wait until you were dead to let me know?" she replied tearfully. The conversation that followed ended nearly five years of communication breakdown as the husband admitted he simply hadn't thought it necessary to speak of the love he felt.

Few relationships could survive long without some sort of re-assurance between the parties involved. A businessman who neglects to show a customer his appreciation, a salesman who never compliments or flatters a buyer, a boss who never says "thanks," would be failures in their attempts to sustain a relationship for any length of time. The poet Emerson said, "Friendships should be kept in constant repair." So should a love affair.

Some ideas. Communication needn't always be verbal. There are dozens of imaginative ways you can speak to your partner without uttering a word. Here are a few; now add some of your own. (Don't let the "she's" mislead you—these are good woman-to-man ideas, too!)

A wink . . . especially during a boring evening, conversation, or meeting. It says, "Wait till we're alone again!"

A smile . . . across a room; in church; when everything's gone wrong; when she looks completely beat and unglamorous. It says, "I'm glad I've got you!"

A kiss . . . when you first wake up or just before you go to sleep; across the table in a restaurant; when she's just done something thoughtful; when she's just failed miserably at something; when her face is dirty or paint-smeared and she feels anything but sexy; to accompany your "thank you's." It says "You still turn me on!"

A pinch . . . right on the bottom! In public or private. It says, "To me you're still the sexiest girl around!"

A touch . . . hold hands; put your arm around her; cup her face in your hands as you kiss her; rub or scratch her back; get "fresh" now and then by brushing your hand across her; help her out of the car; be extra friendly when you help her up the stairs. It says "I find you soft, warm and very enjoyable."

We just don't have time for anything anymore!

Problem. One or both partners are hiding under a lot of unimportant "busy work." People usually end up spending their time where they *want* to spend it. If you don't have time anymore for being together, for lovemaking, or for simply communicating with one another, most likely it's the result of a deeper problem, not the cause of this one.

What to do. Pinpoint the problem and bring it out into the open. Decide between yourselves that you're going to *make* time to solve it. Take time to be together—alone! You can't build anything meaningful between TV commercials, diaper changes, meal preparations, phone conversations, home repair jobs, helping with homework, lodge meetings, bridge clubs, etc. Set aside some time that belongs just to the two of you, time in which you can relax and enjoy each other. When you were dating, you found the time to be together—you simply *made* the time. Do it again!

Nate Benjamin, a prominent therapist and marriage counselor, prescribes weekly 12-hour love-and-talk marathons for couples having difficulty with their marriage and/or sex life. Beginning Sunday morning, as early as possible, the husband and wife are to spend the next 12 hours together doing only two things—talking and loving. They are told to talk about themselves, their marriage, their childhoods, his business—anything that comes to mind and is meaningful. Children are to be sent to the grandparents for the day and there are no distractions allowed: no TV, books, magazines, and no going out for recreation. Couples taking this "treatment" report not only improved sexual relations, but a definite improvement in their communications with each other throughout the week.

Some ideas. Don't rely on just one approach to "taking time" for yourselves; devise a long working list—and use it often. Here are some starters for *your* "brainstorm" list:

Take occasional "second honeymoons" in the quiet luxury of a local hotel. Leave the kids with relatives or friends (and reciprocate later in similar situations for them).

Set aside some "unreachable" time—time when you're simply not available to anyone but each other. No parties, no obligations, no meetings; just yourselves.

Make your day longer! Get up a little earlier or go to bed later. Be sure to use the extra time getting closer to one another.

Don't fight each other for the same time. Give each other some private time to "unwind" after a busy day before turning on the togetherness.

Schedule the kids so they are out of the way for at least a portion of the day. Don't let them be a 24-hour-a-day "excuse."

*He's selfish and inconsiderate—about sex and
everything else!*

Problem. The relationship is in danger because it's becoming one-sided. Selfishness is highly contagious and can spread like the plague from one phase of married life to another. It usually begins with petty matters like choice of entertainment, food, use of time, etc., but once "me" begins to become more important than "you" or "we" in these things, it soon spreads to the larger areas of concern—from choice of friends, furniture, religion, to a couple's sex life and intellectual development.

What to do. Unselfishness and consideration are contagious, too, and everything you do together should include generous portions of these two ingredients. Be quick to realize that what may seem a thoughtless act on the part of your mate may be an unconscious reaction to worry, fear, uncertainty, or just plain old fatigue. Take the initiative; instead of feeling hurt or sorry for yourself, launch a "kindness offensive." This may require some tremendous effort and many creative ideas—but it can have wonderfully positive results.

> When Al Danton came home from work Friday night, he was still miles away mentally, thinking about the annual sales meeting coming up Tuesday. It was the most important meeting in his yearly calendar. His wife, recognizing his need to be free of problems and demands for the next few days, took command. That night the family had a low-key evening. Saturday she took the children visiting so he could work uninterrupted on his reports. Saturday night the family went to a movie together. That night, she got out a new type of liniment and began rubbing her husband's neck. She also took the lead in their sexual relations that evening. The next day, Al slept later while the kids went to Sunday school. In the afternoon, the family went on a picnic. On Monday, the couple was supposed to play bridge, but the wife called and asked to be excused. On Tuesday morning, she fixed her husband's favorite breakfast and sent him off with words of encouragement. The meeting was successful—highly so—and Al came home more relaxed and enthusiastic than she had seen him in months.

In this case, the demands of the husband's business came before the other needs at home temporarily. Both parties undoubtedly realized that on another day the wife would need similar nuturing.

Some ideas. Immediate action is nearly always better than letting a problem like this drag on; face your spouse with your feelings when you feel you're being "neglected," and talk about it. List as many ways as you can of making your mate feel important and loved. Here's a brief starter list:

HIS	HERS
Take over her household duties for a day, or a weekend.	Tell him how nice he looks just before he goes for work.
Serve her breakfast in bed some Sunday.	Don't mess up his newspaper.
Play her favorite game with her and let her win.	Tell him its a good idea even if you think it's stupid.
Talk to her.	Listen!
Open the door for her in public.	Shine his shoes.
Raise her allowance.	Laugh at his jokes.
Hum her favorite song.	Get up and fix his breakfast.
Take your time in bed; give her time to enjoy it too.	Keep yourself trim and attractive even if no one sees you but him.

The only time he/she makes love is when he/she's had something to drink!

Problem. The partner is relying on the artificial instead of the creative to stimulate sexual activity. The use of liquor, drugs, violence, and the like may achieve a certain momentary physical satisfaction but it does nothing for a long-range relationship— except worsen it.

The dynamic person doesn't need this kind of "prop"; there are dozens, even hundreds, of creative methods available for stimulating sexual activity. One good idea is worth a dozen martinis!

What to do. Brainstorm! Prepare a list of as many ways as you can think of to "turn on" your mate. Your list will contain dozens, maybe more, of good usable ideas. Possibly drink or other artificial stimulants might be on the list, but it will be only a small percentage of the total methods available. Just as you wouldn't use the first item on a business brainstorm list without reading and considering the whole list, don't settle for the first method of stimulation that comes to mind. If the first few non-alcoholic ideas don't work, don't rush backwards; keep trying until you click with something.

Some ideas. Use one of the greatest stimulants of all—surprise. Perform some little unexpected act which requires a little added effort on your part. It's an effective way of saying, "You're on my mind at this particular moment in time—because I love you!" Little surprises can act as excellent "turn on's." Here are a few "surprise turn on's" as listed by a group of husbands during a brainstorming session on the subject. See how many you can add to it:

- Give her a *real* kiss when you come home from work tonight.
- Give her a Valentine in January: tell her you couldn't wait any longer.
- Or send one in April: tell her she's *still* your Valentine.
- Tell her you love her as soon as you wake up in the morning.
- Write a love note at the end of her shopping list.
- Play her favorite tune on the stereo—then ask her to dance.
- Put on her favorite after-shave lotion before you go to bed —or better still, shave!
- Kiss her neck or hair when you help her into her coat.

He's thoughtless and doesn't care!

Problem. Believing old wives' tales instead of your heart! "He's thoughtless" is one of the commonest complaints of today's wives, but more often than not he's been given the label unfairly. He isn't that at all; he's simply bought some age-old misconception of how a man should behave in order to prove his masculinity. Smother any marriage with enough "do's and don'ts" and it will quickly become dull instead of dynamic.

What to do. Consider who you really want to impress—"them" or "her." Remember, you have a lifetime contract with "her" and your creative attention to that contract will determine whether your marriage will become a life sentence or a lifetime of satisfaction. One prominent psychiatrist advises husbands to throw away their preconceptions—those handed along by the frustrated, the misinformed or the inexperienced; parents, teachers, sociologists, ministers, even psychologists, are full of taboos regarding marital behavior. Forget them! Or turn on your COMPACT REDUCER and put them in the perspective they deserve. Do what pleases you and your wife; do what enhances your love; ignore the Victorian "masculine" philosophy which makes such deadly claims as these:

It isn't manly to be sentimental.
It isn't proper to show affection in public.
It isn't manly to be clean, well-dressed, and smell good.
You can spoil a woman by being too affectionate to her.
You can best prove your manliness by the number of children you can father.
Infidelity is natural and universal.
Affection is bound to decline as two people grow older.

This kind of masculinity is phony—and dangerous to any relationship. Being thoughtful needn't be such a chore. Oftentimes the simplest act can go the longest way towards brightening up a dull marriage. A little surprise, for example, can be very creative and highly effective. Someone has said that marriage takes all the surprises out of love, and it's true that married couples often replace the excitement of courtship with the drab routine of three-meals-a-day, a clean house, a paycheck, and a movie on Saturday night. But it doesn't *have* to be routine!

Surprise your mate: you'll be surprised at the positive results!

Some ideas. There are plenty of ways a creative husband can surprise his wife (in a positive, loving manner, of course), and there are equally as many ways the favor can (and will) be returned. Let's build your list with these imaginative "starters":

Surprise her with flowers—not on special occasions, but on very "unspecial" days: a gloomy Monday; a rainy day; a report card day; a pretty day; or "just because I love you."
Send her a greeting card that just says "You're pretty special." When it arrives in the bill-laden mail, it will give a lift to the whole day.
Give her some help with the housework; besides being thoughtful, it's good exercise!
When you return from a business trip, bring her something,

even if it's nothing more than a paperback book you picked up in the terminal. It says, "I was thinking of you."

Take the kids off her hands when she's feeling bad. Arrange for her to have some of the peace and quiet she's been yearning for all day.

He never says he loves me!

Problem. One partner is becoming complacent; the other, hard of hearing. In most conversations, repetition becomes monotonous, but in the daily conversation of marriage, the words "I love you" just can't be repeated too often. In their absence, a husband or wife begins feeling insecure, jealous, or taken for granted. A dynamic marriage is one in which love is expressed often. Another problem exists, however, when one partner fails to "hear" the expressions of love which may be transmitted by other than verbal means.

What to do. Say it, show it, prove it—and often! Don't let a single day go by in which you don't remind your spouse of your love. The more imagination you can add to these basic communications, the more effective your reminders will be.

Some ideas. In a recent session with a group of married couples, an Ohio minister asked the question, "How does your husband/wife most effectively say 'I love You'?" Some of their replies can serve as starters for your next brainstorm list:

"By his making the bed in the mornings," was Ruth James' reply. Responding to some surprised looks, she explained. "I realize it's no great chore, yet it's one he doesn't *have* to do—but does. And each time I feel he's telling me, 'Because I love you, I'm willing to help lighten your day's work, even if only a little.' "

"By fixing my favorite meal," replied Ruth's husband, Tom. "She's showing me she not only remembers things that please me, but she's willing to go out of her way to do them. It's a quiet but very effective expression of her love."

"With notes!" was the response of Rob and Bev Warrington. They explained that when either spouse is out late—at meetings, on business, playing bridge,—he leaves a note for the other one on the soap dish. It doesn't list phone calls, problems, or chores to attend in the morning. It simply says, "I love you and I'm glad you're home," with a few endearing embellishments. "It probably sounds silly," says Rob, "but it's nice knowing you were on her mind just before she went to bed."

"By advertising the fact," smiled Rhoda Lawrence. "For our silver anniversary, Harry placed an ad in the classified columns, which read 'I will gladly be responsible for all debts incurred by my beloved wife, Rhoda, as I have happily for the past 25 years and as I hope to for the next 25 years.'"

All we do is argue!

Problem. In spite of the current thinking of some psychologists that fighting is both healthy and essential to a marriage, the fact is that anger and harsh words lead only to more anger and even harsher words, and these are deadly "turn off's." Marital fighting is particularly damaging because of each party's intimate knowledge of his partner's soft spots. Piercing words, spoken in anger, can take weeks, months, or years to extract. Sometimes they can never be.

What to do. Naturally you can't avoid all arguments, but you can use your dynamic abilities to avoid as many as possible, and to more creatively get out of others with a minimum of damage to the relationship. Remember, it takes two to argue. You can avoid many an argument by simply not pressing an issue—especially one that's really not important. Don't quarrel, for example, over insignificant things like names, dates, places, and the exact wording of bygone conversations, even if you feel you're right. Take the advice of the homespun philosopher who offers this advice:

> There's one secret to a happy marriage—
> Whenever you're wrong, admit it
> Whenever you're right—shut up!

When you do argue, watch your language! Don't try to hurt your partner with bitter, cutting words. Treat your mate with at least the same courtesy you'd use in dealing with a business associate, customer, or the next-door neighbor.

Randy and Rita Dyer, realizing how insensitive they had become through their habit of throwing sharp verbal barbs at each other, set up a weekly penalty bank. For every cruel word they spoke to the other, they put in a dime. The proceeds went for "treats"—a movie, dinner out, etc. Within a month the bank was empty. There are occasional lapses, but for the most part they cured themselves of a potentially disastrous habit by recognizing that words can prompt hatred as well as love.

Learn to laugh together more—and you'll fight less. Love is supposed to be fun, too, and when it ceases to be fun and a man and woman stop laughing at and with each other, the relationship loses something vital. Laughter—good, sincere, appreciative laughter—can be sexy as well as a good communications bridge. It's a pleasant way of saying, "I'm enjoying your company—and you!" Actor Richard Burton says:

> I'd rather hear a girl laugh well than to try to turn me on with long, silent, soulful secret looks. If you can laugh with a woman, everything else falls into place.

Some ideas. Prepare a list of ways in which you can improve your relationship by making it a happier, more positive one. It might include some of these suggestions:

List all the points on which you two agree . . . and refer to it often.

List "unimportant topics" and agree to stop arguing about them.

Always resolve your argument before you go to sleep.

See that your entertainment includes occasional funny movies, plays, or musical comedies.

Develop some verbal argument stoppers (like "You're cute when you're mad") and use them to divert your partner's anger.

Clip cartoons, jokes, funny news articles, which might have some relevance to your relationship and laugh at them together.

Develop and share lots of "private jokes."

He's/she's become a real slob—hard even to be around!

Problem. The chase is over, and one or both parties decides the relationship no longer needs the physical glamour required in courtship. Many a marriage has quickly cooled off because one or both parties simply let themselves go from the standpoint of appearance and personal hygiene. Such situations frequently lead to irritating nagging on the part of the husband or wife, a lessening of physical contact, embarrassment in being seen together, or outright rejection.

What to do. The years aren't always kind, but they needn't be too damaging either. A recognition of the problem and a tactful, creative approach to it can have long-lasting results. Sometimes gentle hints will work; sometimes the "we" approach will do the job ("I'm putting on a little weight—will you go on a diet with me and help me stick with it?"); sometimes, however, more cleverness is required, as in this case:

> After several years of marriage, Ruth Wilson found her husband getting neglectful about his person, something she recognized could easily cause an indifference to the romantic part of living together. She solved her problem with a clever switch in their usual relationship. She made a game of being the "aggressor." She would slip him a note, for example, which read "Brush your teeth, take a shower, and meet me in the bedroom in half an hour." Or, following dinner, she would run his bath, lay out his pajamas and tell him, "Relax and soak in a nice warm tub while I put the kids to bed." She always told him how irresistible he was when he wore a new cologne or lotion. The "game" worked, the marriage improved, and now her husband even writes her a note occasionally.

> Miles Taswell was becoming disturbed about his wife's increasingly sloppy personal appearance. Basically an attractive woman, she seldom combed her hair, was beginning to put on weight, and seemed to be giving little thought to the way she dressed. He consulted a psychologist friend for advice on how to handle the problem. "One reason," his friend said, "a woman lets herself get run-down looking is because she often has no reason for looking otherwise. Take her out on the town regularly—that'll mean she has to fix herself up regularly. Give her a reason for staying attractive and she will." At the time, money was tight and Miles didn't feel he could afford round after round of "weekend" dining, so he hit upon a less expensive but effective plan. Frequently throughout the year, he invited his wife in from the suburbs to lunch with him in a nice restaurant. She welcomed not only the chance to dress up, but also the opportunity to escape the boredom of house-wifery and to discuss things in an air-con-

ditioned, relaxed atmosphere with her husband. The outings improved both her appearance and their married life.

Some ideas. When you receive compliments from others about his/her appearance, pass them on. Call her beautiful (or him handsome); she/he will try harder to live up to it. Shower together; give him/her a scented rubdown afterwards. Set aside a larger allowance in her budget for new clothes, hairdos, etc.

We have nothing in common anymore!

Problem. A definite lack of creative effort in *trying* to find some common interests. No matter how unlike two people may be, there is always something for them to share. The problem is simply deciding to solve the problem and determining where to start.

What to do. If you have difficulty settling on a large, long-range common interest (such as bridge-playing, writing, art, redecorating, theatre-going, collecting, golf, travel), look for several "little" one-time events in which you can practice togetherness (put in a patio, paint the house, go bike-riding, buy a new home). You can find common interests, too, in day-to-day things such as sharing a favorite magazine, newspaper, book, or TV program.

The old saying "don't knock it if you haven't tried it" is good advice in fighting this particular problem. You may find that your interests are more common than you thought if you merely join your spouse in his or her interests. Here's an example:

> Keith and Bobbie Simmons had a problem. He was an avid football fan and watched the pro games on TV by the hour. Bobbie felt neglected but complaints only led to arguments. So she reached a solution as old as history: "If you can't fight 'em, join 'em!" She began reading the sport page, learning players' names and abilities, studying the rules, and finally herself became an avid pro football fan. Now she and Keith watch together and have many exciting moments in sports to recap during the weekdays. "It's done wonders for our marriage," Bobbie said, "and when you get down to it, football's a lot more stimulating than the latest gossip at the ladies' guild!"

Sometimes it helps to choose some neutral ground for establishing the common interest so that neither party is giving in to the other in order to promote togetherness. For example, you might take a course in adult education together—something you'll both enjoy, but which is neither party's "bag."

> Jerry and Tina Larkin enrolled together in a class on sculpting. Instead of sculpting a likeness of the professional model, however, they decided to do busts of each other. "The results were amazing," Jerry reported. "For the first time in our marriage we really began looking at each other: I mean really exploring each other's facial features and discussing what it was about the other that most attracted us. By the time we finished the course we had become much closer. We also had two rather professional-looking busts of one another—permanent reminders of a very special period in our lives."

Try breaking a bad habit together. If you both smoke, discuss and implement ways to give up—or at least cut down. If you both have a weight problem, help each other overcome it.

Some ideas. Share excitement, and perhaps a little danger, together. Many of the strongest human relationships are formed in times of great stress or danger. If you can't go skydiving or big game hunting together, at least share some "scary" moments such as driving on a treacherous mountain road, or riding in a roller coaster, or flying in a private plane together. Explore a cave; get lost in a large city; talk back to a head waiter; go camping together. Learn to ski or ice-skate together. Teach her how to drive. Explore a haunted house; see a horror movie together. Take in a boxing or wrestling match and root for the "bad guy."

Do something new together—often! The more experiences you can share, the closer your relationship becomes; and the closer it becomes, the more relaxed and intense your sexual relationship can be.

Our sex life has become more a chore than a pleasure!

Problem. The "chore" feeling arises when sex is approached without the right kind of buildup and pre-play. When this happens, you're saying "Let's hurry up and get it over with," when you should be saying, "This is wonderful—let's enjoy it to the fullest!"

What to do. Make your buildup more than just a few quick passes and whispered words. Build toward the sex act through your conversation, actions, and overall relationship. Make your love a total, not just a sexual relationship, and you'll find "making love" much more than just an expression.

An effective put-down in marriage is "Not now—there isn't time." That's usually all it is, though—a put-down. Stop and analyze the great American hurry habit and you find that our mad rush from one place to another is often just an excuse we use to keep from facing each other and communicating as we should. When you come down to it, what's the hurry, really? Take time to make the sex act more meaningful and rewarding. Show one another that your relationship is more important than being on time to the Joneses, the movies, a bridge game, or anything else at the moment.

A "quickie" is fun now and then, but to make a regular practice of "instant sex" is merely getting it over with. Take time to talk, explore, stimulate, and to experiment.

Some ideas: A group of young couples were asked recently to list as many things as they could think of which they considered sexy and stimulating to their marriage. Here are a few items from their lists. Why not add more of your own to it?

Go to an X-rated movie together and sit through it twice.

Have the local evening disc jockey dedicate a song to her from you.

Read a racy novel together, each taking an alternate chapter and telling the other about it.

Hold hands in church.

Install a full-length mirror in your bedroom.

Pay her a compliment in front of friends, particularly other women.

Help her out of the car and stare at her legs as you do.

Go swimming on a private beach—with or without suits.

Take her to a Playboy Club and make disparaging remarks about the Bunny's figure.

Refer to her as "my girlfriend," "my mistress," or "my bride" in front of a hotel clerk.

Buy her some sheer, lacy pajamas or nightgown for her birthday. It's a nice way of saying, "Who cares about the year you've added—you're still sexy to me!"

Kiss her wedding ring.

225 IDEAS—NOW PUT THEM TO WORK!

In this chapter we've listed over 225 different ideas for making your marriage more meaningful and your personal life more satisfying. Is that all it takes?

Not really. All the marriage manuals ever written, all the marriage counsellors, psychiatrists, and ministers ever licensed, all the newspaper and magazine columns on the subject of marriage—all of them combined can't accomplish a thing in a man-woman relationship *unless* the two people involved want it to. If you really, sincerely want to improve your relationship with your lifetime partner, the principles of dynamic, creative thinking can and will help you.

Remember, you must first define whatever problem is preventing your relationship from being all it should. It may be considerably more complicated than those we've covered in this chapter. It may involve other personalities such as in-laws, children, friends, or other persons. But remember, a problem is still a problem, and by facing up to it, isolating it, and working on it creatively, you can and will be able to solve it. Discuss it with your lover and brainstorm possible solutions to the problem. It may not always work the first time or second time you try it; you may get only one good idea out of every 25, but a good idea in marriage can have lifelong results.

Be a totally dynamic person. Don't restrict your creative activities to the job alone. Be prepared to use it in every phase of your marriage, too. You'll be pleased to discover how effective your partner can help make you in return. A dynamic personality means a more dynamic marriage, which in turn means *two* happy and dynamic personalities. Is it worth the investment? Of course it is. Doubly worth it!

IDEAS FOR A DYNAMIC MARITAL AND PERSONAL LIFE

Turn your idea generators loose again and see how many ideas you can come up with for making your marital and personal life more exciting and more meaningful. Jot down on a sheet of paper ways you could pleasantly surprise your mate tonight; six ways you could stop the next argument you have; six suggestions for improving your communications with each other; six ways you can save more time for spending with each other; six new things you could do together this weekend; six common experiences you could share together during the weeks ahead; six new ways you might more effectively stimulate your partner; six unique and exciting things you could get for your partner's birthday.

Do more than make your lists: put them into action. And the sooner the better—for both of you!

12

Turning Boredom into Dynamic Activity!

Boredom is the seed of all creativeness.

Eric Hoffer

Well, we've made it! After centuries of striving to improve our social, working, living and health conditions so we might have enough time and money to really enjoy life, we've actually reached our goal. Today we have more leisure time than any generation since Adam. But it's also possible that we're the most bored generation since Adam.

The working man is bored because he is no longer required to work to his capacity. Much of his thinking is done by computer and most of his physical work by machine. As the challenge of his work declines, so does his interest—and if he isn't in a job that interests him, he may spend decades in a state of complete boredom and frustration.

The housewife is bored. Much of the creativity of homemaking has been eliminated by modern technology. She has no more soap to make, no more tomatoes to can, no quilts to quilt, no clothes to design and make. Now, from sunrise to sunset, all she has to do is "push buttons." Not much drudgery—but lots of boredom.

Young people are bored. Reared on a steady diet of TV, they feel they have already seen everything and done everything. They become suspicious and cynical. They tend to drag around or rush about without really caring. They become apathetic—often lacking purpose, direction, and dedication. They provide lots of noise and movement, but they actually enjoy very little of it.

But this is far from being as grim as it sounds. Boredom *is* deadly and braindulling—for some people. But for the dynamic person, it is another creative catalyst—often one of the most effective!

For the imaginative mind, there's a definite cause-effect relationship between the words "Ho-hum" and "I've got an idea!" Boredom is an uncomfortable, even painful feeling, and man has often gone to great creative lengths to combat it. It was this that led Ralph Linton to remark, "The human capacity for being bored, rather than man's social or natural needs, lies at the root of man's cultural advance."

It's important, then, for the development of your dynamic personality to know, understand and respect boredom as you would a formidable competitor. Be prepared to tackle any ho-hum activity as a creative challenge, using your vast storehouse of creative tools and techniques.

What are the symptoms of boredom? They might best be summed up in this psychiatrist's report to some distraught parents who felt their teenager was in need of clinical help:

> Patient exhibits frequent fatigue, constant drowsiness, high susceptibility to sickness, continual grouchiness, crossness and impatience, universal disinterest in the world around him, and an almost complete withdrawal from all but the simplest mental activity. In short, he's bored to death!

The doctor prescribed large and frequent doses of creative activities. What causes boredom? Four things, say the psychologists.

1. Great amounts of uncommitted time with no plan for using it in a stimulating manner.
2. Repetition. Getting into a rut doing anything from the mundane acts of eating, dressing, or rising, to your job or the way you commute to it.
3. A moral or philosophical life pattern that doesn't allow for continuous change. A country philosopher said once, "Whenever I meet a feller who says he hasn't changed his views in the last 25 years, I'm always glad he's more liberal about his socks."
4. Approaching *anything* in a way that's less than creative.

Boredom in action (or in-action). A lecturer on Creative Dynamics recently asked his audience to brainstorm with him for a few minutes to compile a "ho-hum" list—things they considered terribly boring. He used the list to demonstrate how nearly all the things people consider boring are things *they need not put up with.* They can, by simply using their imaginations and their own dynamic personalities, eliminate their own personal ho-hum lists. Here are some excerpts from the brainstorm:

HO-HUM LIST

Watching TV on vacation

Watching TV—period

Spending Saturday evening home

Sitting through "entertainment" you don't enjoy

Playing with someone who always wins

Taking a vacation where you *have* to go instead of where you want to go

A dull party

Most political speeches

Going shopping with a woman

Conversation with a drunk

Home movies (other people's)

Talking about the weather

Listening to people talk about their children

Most meetings

Doing something you don't like

Serving on committees where you have no say

Doing housework

Reading a dull book—required reading

Being told something you already know

Listening to a self-made man

Waiting in line—for anything

Having the same thing for breakfast every day

Not understanding what's being said

Sustained conversation with children

Hearing the same story for the umpteenth time

Notice how these "ho-hums" fall into four general areas of boredom: entertainment, work, outside activities, and daily routine. Using these categories as a guide, on the following pages we'll explore ways you can turn some of the more common "ho-hums" into "I've got an idea!"

Ho-Hum—What'll We Do This Weekend?

Here's something that comes up 52 times a year. The perpetually bored person will reply, "Oh, I dunno—rake leaves and watch TV, I guess." The dynamic person, on the other hand, will work at making these 48-hour "vacations" stimulating and useful and will respond in a variety of ways.

Have a party! Not just one of those parties where everyone dresses in uncomfortable clothes to drink and chatter away the evening. Throw an unusual party! Make it an exciting one that you and your guests will talk about for a long time. Put your imagination to work: you'll find dozens of interesting approaches.

Vary the nature of the party. Don't limit yourself to the "usual"; try dances, costume parties, dinner parties, theatre parties, swimming parties, wine-tasting parties, card parties, or even work parties.

> One couple moved into a house which they planned to redecorate, so they invited friends to a paint-in. Guests were allowed to draw, write, or paint anything they wished on the walls. Some wrote graffiti, some wrote limericks, some painted murals, some played word games. All had a completely enjoyable, relaxing time.

Vary the location. Try progressive dinners, barn-dances, a Halloween party in a haunted house, or outdoor events such as clambakes, weiner roasts, barbecues. You might even have fun simply holding your party in a different part of the house.

> A suburban housewife, Collette Cooper, gave a party to christen her newly-remodeled bathroom. She served punch from the washbowl and appetizers from a tray in the bath tub; decorative bathroom tissue was used for napkins. It was fun and a great conversation piece for months to come.

Vary the motif. Build your party around the theme and add excitement to it. Consider ideas like the Roaring Twenties, World War II, the Fabulous Forties, occult parties (complete with a palm reader), election parties, brainstorm parties, or something built around a foreign theme—Spanish, Italian, Swiss, French, Japanese.

Mrs. Al Frank, known in her circle of friends as one of New England's best cooks of Italian foods, pulled a switch one night and threw a Swiss party, with fondue as a main dish. She even used Swiss travel posters for decorations and spoke a little French as she served the meal.

Vary the time. Why limit your parties to the evening? Have a breakfast or brunch; start the party in the mid-afternoon. Be flexible. As a surprise switch for her son's 14th birthday, one mother invited a group of his friends over at 5:30 a.m. for a candlelight breakfast. Another creative wife invited some friends for a Sunday champagne brunch, topped with a rented full-length movie featuring silent film comedians.

Enjoyment, not the hour, is important when it's party time!

Build, remodel or repair something. Throw yourself into projects that will have some useful, eye-catching, or lasting value. Use your creative and constructive talents to beautify your surroundings or make everyday life more convenient.

In the early days of her marriage, Kay Boswell purchased second-hand furniture and antiqued it. Now she can afford new things but prefers to continue buying period pieces and completely refinishing them. It's a useful way to spend her time in a creative, constructive fashion, and she also has furniture worth many times its purchase price.

The grandfather of Charles Young left 100 acres of tree-covered land to be used as a public park. When the city was unable to appropriate enough funds to fix up the property with paths, benches, access roads, and the like, Charles decided to take matters into his own hands—literally. He obtained permission from the city to pitch a tent within the park and to do as much "remodeling" work as he was able, and he spent his entire four-week vacation with his family working over the area with axes, chainsaws, rakes, etc. His reward: the satisfaction of seeing a park "grow," plus about a three-year supply of firewood from the trees he cut.

Go on an outing! Get out of the house and go on a picnic, a family retreat, a fruit-picking expedition with your spouse; hunting or fishing with your son, friends, or both; a shopping spree, a boatride, anything that takes you into the fresh air for a while.

One couple goes on periodic househunting "sprees," even though it may be some time before they're ready to buy a new house. They enjoy the stimulation of comparing different floor-plans, furnishings, techniques, and other home improvement ideas as well as the anticipation of owning their own home some day.

A favorite family outing for the Walsh family is a "coin-toss" ride. The whole gang piles into the car and off they go. Each time they come to an intersection, they flip a coin. Heads means they turn left, tails, right. The result is usually some wild but interesting rides. Not surprisingly, the coin usually guides them by an ice cream stand, resulting in treats for the whole family.

Get a group together! Join forces with other people who enjoy interesting and unusual activities and pool ideas with them. Form adult discussion groups, a revolving "potluck" group, or a junior-sized travel club. The more the merrier!

A bowling club for couples decided, after two years of bowling together, that they were in a rut, and agreed to vary their enter-tainment activities. Now it's something different each month—a play, a concert, dinner out, hitting nightspots, horseraces, etc. They even go bowling once a year!

Another group formed a "party of the month club" in which they take turns throwing unusual celebrations of off-beat events. They may honor Groundhogs Day, National Pickle Week, the Firing on Ft. Sumpter, or the birthday of Millard Fillmore—any excuse for getting together and having fun.

Ho-Hum—What'll We Do For Vacation This Year?

Vacation is the one time of year set aside for enjoyment, so why not use it for that? Don't consider it a time for fulfilling obliga-tions ("We went to your mother's house last year—this year we'll visit my mother"), or for trying to keep up with or top the Joneses ("They went to Florida, so *we'll* go to the Bahamas"). Pick the kind of place and activities you really want; don't saddle yourself with a lot of dull days doing something you don't particularly en-joy just because it goes under the heading of recreation. Put *idea additives* into your vacation this year!

Do something different! If you own a plot of vacationland somewhere, don't tie yourself down to it year after year. Trade sites occasionally with someone else who owns a plot in an entirely different location. Join a travel club. It serves as an enforced saving program and can save you a considerable amount of money on "expensive" type vacations via group rates and other discounts. You'll end up with some exotic vacations, too, all over the world. Spend your vacation money creatively; don't fritter it away on the ordinary.

Every other year, Marv and Dot Hill "shoot the works" on a dream trip. Instead of spreading their savings out over the full three-week vacation, they spend one week in a very lush, expensive, interesting location: Rome, Paris, Las Vegas, New York. The remaining weeks they call the "poverty vacation," and have fun via free or inexpensive creative activities within driving range of home.

Plan something you can continue throughout the year! Stretch your vacation enjoyment by making it a learning experience. Learn a new skill, take up a new hobby, develop a new interest—one which can be done anywhere.

Tess Robbins signed up for an art course while vacationing in New England, and learned to do oil painting. The natural beauty of the ocean and surrounding countryside provided her with plenty of inspiring settings, and the resulting paintings were attractive reminders of a pleasant summer. She didn't put her enjoyment in mothballs, however; she continued painting and soon began doing well enough at it to enter her work in various local exhibits.

Try something that can lead to a career or new interests. If you're not completely satisfied in your job, use vacation time for exploring other possibilities. If you think you want to be a writer, spend your vacation at a writer's conference and investigate the requirements and rewards with faculty and fellow students. If politics is your dream, take a vacation in Washington, D.C. and see it in action. If you have a hobby, use your vacation to broaden it.

An executive with a long-standing interest in sailing decided to give that a try one summer, so he bought an old boat and fixed it up. One day he was asked if he would consider renting his boat. He did, and launched himself into a boat-rental business. To protect his investment, he began giving sailing lessons; then he began arranging elaborate sailing vacations and weekends; and now he has a profitable full-time business in a field where he is happiest—boating.

Vacations can open doors to an unlimited variety of interests, the kind which you can continue to develop long past the summertime.

The Edwards family uses each vacation as the starting point of a new area of research. Some years they take a historical trip, studying up on events, then seeing for themselves where the events actually happened. They do the same with geology and folklore. The kids love the thrill of learning and the parents, both teachers, follow through with research papers on the subjects.

Do something worthwhile! Put your vacation time to use helping others, or in some way furthering your social, political, or religious beliefs. Help in summer camps for the underprivileged, volunteer for your church's summertime efforts in some inner city ghettos; take city children to country events such as state fairs or farms; give the elderly a hand on their vacations; use your talents and your ideas in a positive, worthwhile fashion.

HOLIDAYS FOR HUMANITY is an organization founded by an Indiana dermatologist with an interest in Central and South America. It arranges for physicians, dentists, nurses, and medical technicians to spend their vacations (without pay and at their own expense) helping the sick and needy in various backward regions of these Latin countries. Those who go seldom return physically relaxed, but they always come back emotionally refreshed.

Make this vacation—and the next and the next—a dynamic one. Fill it with ideas, creative projects, and fun, and you'll find yourself rewarded in many ways.

Ho-Hum—The Weather's Lousy; Now What Do We Do?

The weather often becomes a convenient fall guy as an excuse for inactivity and resultant boredom—but not for the dynamic person. Neither rain nor storm nor gloom, etc., should prevent you from putting your time and the elements to creative use.

Try outdoor sports! Don't hide from snowy or freezing weather; take advantage of it! Learn to ski or ice skate; build a snowman or snow fort (it's still fun no matter how old you are); go sledding or tobogganing; go for hikes; give the birds and wildlife a break by building them some feeders.

> One rugged Vermont city dweller turns the frequent heavy snows into a clever form of outdoor-indoor recreation. Each winter he builds an igloo—one large enough for adults to stand up inside and strong enough for children to slide down on. His igloo is so well-constructed and heavy that it is the last piece of ice to melt in the spring. Adult friends and neighbors are invited over for hot chocolate or hot bourbon by candlelight in the igloo. By winter's end he has made many new acquaintances via his "igloo parties."

Try indoor sports! When the weather outside is *too* frightful, don't just race for the TV—consider some indoor creative activities. If you're with someone of the opposite sex, you need no further advice. But if you are stormed in as family, turn to some creative family activities: Start a construction project (build a recreation room or work area); take a trip down memory lane with a photo album or some old phonograph records; tell stories to one another (some great pieces of literature were born this way, including Mary Shelly's *Frankenstein*); break out some games (Monopoly, Chinese Checkers, etc.)

> During the worst storm of the year, Evelyn Ingram decided to turn the family recreation room into a Las Vegas casino, complete with roulette wheel and other card-and-chip devices. The family made it an all-day experience with chips and winnings redeemable for cookies and other snacks. The day passed quickly and, in terms of fun, everybody was a winner!

Ho-Hum—Another Day, Another Dollar!

Keeping busy doesn't necessarily prevent you from being bored. In fact, it's been said that "the most serious idleness of all is being busy with things that do not matter." Just because your present job keeps you occupied eight or more hours a day you're not guaranteed relief from boredom.

Do something you like! Don't hold onto a job after it ceases being interesting or stimulating to you. Look around. Are you uncomfortable on an indoor job? Take an outdoor one. Don't settle back into a semi-comfortable state of boredom until you're 65. Decide on "your thing," then do it!

> David Pike decided to move outdoors and to trade a lucrative but confining middle management job for an outside one that offered him practically unlimited freedom. He applied for the position of caretaker of the county camping grounds on an island in Washington, a job which pays only $100 per month, plus free rent and utilities, but which provides him with a great deal of spare time. He has planned many creative income-producing as well as leisure activities for that time, as well as building a new caretaker's home from materials supplied by the county. He and his family are fully enjoying their move from the rat race to the "rugged life."

Make the job more interesting! Fill it with idea additives; try new ways of doing everything you do, of saving time or energy, of making it more profitable. Accept new tasks willingly and attack them creatively. Consider new ways of improving relations with everyone with whom you come in daily contact.

> Bernard Valdes was disturbed when he overheard his boss refer to him as "a good man, but terribly negative," so he decided to overcome what had apparently become a bad habit—that of saying "no" and "it can't be done." He vowed that, for the next 24 hours, he would say "yes" to every suggestion, question, instruction, or order that came his way. He had to grit his teeth a few times, but he stuck with it and was pleasantly surprised at the positive effect it had on his co-workers and the boss.
> When his pretty redhaired secretary questioned him about his dramatic change in personality, he confided his secret to her. A few days later she told him that she had followed his example and set aside the previous day as a "yes" day—24 hours of answering "yes" to every suggestion she received. She refused to discuss the results (other than those related to her job), and added, "I'll think twice before I do *that* again!"

Make the place you work more interesting. A frequent comment of employees is "I like the job, but it's such a dull place to work." Then liven it up! Without turning a place of business into a college campus or weekend party, there are many good, creative ways to make your workday more interesting.

Tiring of frequent office collections for birthday gifts for each person, the people in one large office decided on a different approach. Instead of the group treating each individual on his or her birthday, the role would be reversed and the "birthday person" would bring in treats for the whole department to devour on breaktime. It cuts down on expenses, yet provides several dozen "break parties" a year.

Ho-Hum—Guess I'll Take a Nap; There's Nothing Else to Do

Life is short enough; don't sleep it away! Naturally, when you're tired you should rest or take a snooze, but don't use it as an excape from boredom. That's a "cop-out" and a deadly one, according to a British doctor who claims that the healthiest, happiest, most successful and intelligent people are those who make do with a minimum amount of sleep—about five hours a night. "More than that," he says, "is a bad habit and dulls the brain!" Keep your brain alive and active by being alive and active yourself.

Take up a hobby! Collect, build, make, paint, look, walk, travel —do whatever you enjoy and what keeps you alert. Try stamp collecting. Besides providing you with an interesting and profitable collection, it makes the daily mail more exciting as you watch for new commemorative stamps. The same with coin collecting. It makes each pocketful of change a mine of excitement. There are unlimited things to collect: pictures, books, antiques, matchbooks, models, historical objects, figurines, graffiti, headstone tracings, chess sets—in fact, anything that exists is fair game.

Norm Tenney, a traveling man, collects barns—in photographs, of course. He finds when he's driving that watching for a quaint photographic barn he can stop and shoot with his camera keeps him alert. Since he began his hobby, his photography has improved to such an extent that his collection has been exhibited in and around his home town.

Pat McCorkle, a housewife, decided to take up "spelunking" and joined a group of explorers in a cave near her Alabama home. Besides having some thrilling underground experiences, she has supplemented her income by writing articles about caves and explorations for local papers and magazines.

Read! Philosopher Van Horne said, "If one does not read books, how is the mind to cope with solitude? What sort of interior monologue can a non-reader conjure up on a gray day?" Read for pleasure as well as education and use what you read to stimulate your imagination.

Read something you wouldn't ordinarily read. If you're not a Shakespeare fan, read one of his plays. It may not change your tastes but it will stir the cobwebs in your mind and expose you to some different thinking. When you read only those newspapers whose editorial policies you agree with, magazines you enjoy, books that turn you on, you miss some excellent reading.

Rotate the type of book you read; for each novel you read, read a self-improvement book. For every story with a happy ending, read one with an unhappy one. Read your newspaper with a purpose in mind—hunt for ideas. See what you can clip to send with your next letter home. What cartoon or article would be interesting on the bulletin board? What news event is worth a good strong letter to the editor? What might prompt a letter to your congressman? What might stimulate some new interests and ideas for your youngsters? What would make some good conversation starters at lunch—or your next call? Treat each newspaper or magazine as a treasurehouse of ideas.

Write! If you have some creative writing talent, bring it forth and start doing something with it. Take courses in writing; study proven techniques and devices found in books and magazines on writing, and put them to use. Even if you're not qualified to write the great American novel, you can at least write letters—interesting ones, controversial ones, humorous ones. When you run out of things to say in your letters, start doing *new* things to write about! Keep a diary. Write letters or cards to the "forgotten people"— the aged, the sick, overseas servicemen.

Harriet Bennett was dismayed when she read a letter from a young GI who was later killed in Vietnam, in which he said, "It seems like we're forgotten over here—no one seems to care." So she started an organization called "We *Do* Care" in which she and her friends publish a newsletter, write personal letters, and send packages to the boys from their hometown who are overseas. The many complimentary letters she and her group have received attest to the effectiveness of these communications on the morale of the troops, but Harriet insists that "I get more out of this than they do!" Perhaps she does, in the form of creative fulfillment and an absence of boredom.

Ho-Hum—Even the Newspapers Are Dull These Days

So liven them up! Get yourself active in government and use your ideas and efforts to improve your city, state, or nation. If you have the personality for it, run for public office; if you're more the "back up" type, then back up honest, creative candidates. There are dozens of ways you can help them in their campaigns —and with a little brainstorming you can add several dozen more. If you're the agitator type, then agitate—but do it in a positive, creative manner.

Ho-Hum—I'm So Lonely!

Being alone needn't be synonomous with loneliness. As one elderly lady put it, "I have spent many a day alone, but never a lonely day!" There are many dynamic people who are, of necessity, alone a great deal of the time, but who make creative use of their solitude.

Make friends—the dynamic kind! When you're alone and plagued by loneliness, the last thing in the world you need is to be surrounded by self-pitying, self-centered people whose preoccupation with boredom could become contagious. Make it a point to be around people who are alive and active, who will feed you new, exciting ideas, and who can help you act on yours. Form discussion groups with friends, neighbors, even children if they are old enough to understand. Keep in touch with long-distance friends by letters, phone calls, or visits.

Recruit others! Battling boredom can't be a solo activity. You need the help and encouragement of others, especially those closest to you. Sell the principles of dynamic thinking to your mate, your friends, co-workers, fraternal associates—anybody who can contribute to making your life interesting. If they're not on your side, they can dampen your enthusiasm by being wet blankets. When you finish reading this book, give it to your mate, a friend, or a co-worker and expose them to the creative techniques you've learned. Don't be put off by a negative or indifferent attitude; if you don't succeed at first, try different approaches.

> Shortly after his 25th anniversary, Ed Dowley gave notice to his wife that he was finished with the dull life they'd been leading and from then on he was planning to break away from the routine and live: he would travel, go places, see things and do things without worrying about practicality or what the neighbors might think. He invited his wife to join him, but stated that with or without her, he intended to "get going." His wife responded to the ultimatum and joined him—and to her amazement, enjoyed it. Their life together is now an active, dynamic one, free from the hundreds of invisible restrictions they had placed on it previously.

Ho-Hum—Same Old Routine

If the old routine is lulling you to sleep standing up, change it! No part of your daily routine should be considered too insignificant to change. Variety in even the smallest habit can be healthy and productive. Always keep yourself thinking about better, more interesting methods of doing everything.

Eat, drink, and be dynamic! Our oft-repeated advice to "eat something different" needn't mean dining out every night, consuming caviar for lunch, or serving sour herring for breakfast. It can mean such simple variations as putting salt instead of sugar on your grapefruit (or vice-versa), having Grape-nuts instead of Wheaties, trying a new salad dressing, putting catsup instead of mustard on your hotdog, or adding mushrooms to your spaghetti sauce. If you're a drinker, be a creative one. Don't become a permanent Scotch and soda or dry martini drinker. Vary your order; try the specialty of the house wherever you go. You will discover many unusual and tasty combinations.

Let getting there be half the fun! Commuting to and from work can represent a tremendous amount of unproductive time every week, or it can become a stimulating, useful time of day for you. Put some variety into your route, your mode of transportation, or what you do during the ride. Don't turn off your mind while you ride—use it!

Brainstorm with your car pool: try solving problems regarding work, traffic, social interest, home maintenance, traveling, etc.

Use a cassette or dictaphone and record your morning memos or reports on the way in.

If you commute by train or bus, read a book or study a new subject instead of burying yourself in the morning paper.

Play word games—Twenty Questions, Password, etc.

Make waiting worthwhile! Standing in line—for anything, anywhere—can be boring beyond belief unless you use the time creatively. If you're by yourself, take along a book to read or stationery for writing a letter; if you're with someone, brainstorm; listen to others in line and use their comments or conversations to spark ideas.

Phil Herschel, a free-lance greeting card writer, was standing in a long line waiting to get into a movie. Up ahead some teenagers were exchanging the latest jokes with one another. He began writing them down, and when he got home converted several into clever humorous card ideas. He more than paid for the evening's entertainment when he sold two of the ideas to the first editor he sent the material to.

Ho-Hum—People Are So Boring

There's really no such thing as a boring person; those people we often label boring are simply people with whom we haven't yet learned to communicate. Learn to communicate creatively; learn to listen creatively, too, and you'll never be considered boring yourself. Once this happens, you'll have to go a long way to find a really boring person.

Ho-Hum or Away We Go!—It's Really Up to You, Isn't It?

If boredom creeps into your life and makes it anything less than the enjoyable, productive one you deserve, you have only one person to complain to. Yourself. Look over your personal "ho-hum" list once again. Are there any things on it that you are *really* unable to control? Few, if any! Ho-hum activities can't remain ho-hum for very long if you turn loose your imagination on them.

—Keep your dynamic personality active 24 hours a day.
—Use your creative tools to come up with interesting and exciting ideas.
—Put unproductive time to some stimulating use.
—Stay out of ruts; avoid repetition of anything that can be done another way.
—Develop a philosophy of life that promotes activity rather than stagnation.

Remember, the choice between a boring day-to-day existence or a rich, full, dynamic life is strictly up to you!

IDEAS FOR BATTLING BOREDOM

Make your own Ho-Hum list. Jot down on a sheet of paper six or more activities (or inactivities) which you consider boring and uncreative. Now, for each item you've just listed, write down three or more ways you can make that activity more exciting or more constructive. Use your creative power tools to help you on this one. Be prepared to enlarge, reduce, adapt, and so on.

Do some more idea generation. List six or more ideas under each of these questions:

How can I make my next vacation more stimulating?

What can I do this weekend that's different and interesting?

Who do I know that would make an interesting discussion group?

How can I make my job more interesting?

What can I read this week that's interesting and different?

13

Making the Dynamic Way a Habit

Good habits are the soul's muscles. The more you use them, the stronger they grow.

Anon.

If you're an average reader, you've spent just a little over four hours reading this book so far. In it, over a thousand people have shown you, through their own experiences, how to develop your dynamic personality through a more complete and frequent use of your imagination and creative powers. Also, by now you've had numerous opportunities to put the principles outlined in this book to work for you, solving problems and becoming a more effective, more alive person. You've seen for yourself the vital difference a creative approach can make to everything you do. You've no doubt been pleased, at times, with the results. Satisfied, too.

Don't be! This is only the beginning. In these four hours of reading, we've done little more than show you a drop in the bucket. Your mental abilities and creative powers are many, many times more powerful than you yet realize. The hidden treasure within you might be compared to those in this recent incident in Sicily:

Two burglars were thanked for discovering a hidden treasure that the owner of a villa didn't even realize he posesssed. The thieves broke open an unused wall safe and were in the process of making a speedy getaway with its contents—$320,000 in cash—when they were caught by police. When the owner was notified that the police had recovered the money, the man was completely (but happily) surprised. The safe had been locked since the death of his father and he had not been able to open it for over 20 years and was unaware of its contents. He asked the police to convey his gratitude to the thieves for making the discovery.

This book probably won't help you stumble onto that kind of monetary fortune, but hopefully it *has* helped you make an even more important discovery—of those dynamic powers within you which have long been waiting to be detected and brought into play.

Now it's up to you to take it from here, to make the use of these newly unlocked dynamic forces a *habit*. Getting ideas is a lot like eating popcorn: once you get started you'll find it's almost impossible to stop. Creative thought can be habit forming—if you work at it! In this, our final chapter, we want to help you turn yourself into a creature of habit—the dynamic kind!

THE ANATOMY OF A HABIT

There are three things a habit (good *or* bad) must have in order to develop properly:

1. *A need or a reward.* These can be either physical or emotional. A physical need might be for an outlet for energy, activity, or pleasure. The emotional need could range from the desire for security or escape to the need for attention or reassurance.
2. *A starter stimulant.* There must be something to trigger the habit each time it's brought into play. This stimulant could be a person, place, or thing.
3. *Repetition.* Repeat anything often enough and you'll soon be able to do it automatically. Once a routine is established, it is very difficult to break.

Take a few minutes and apply these three facts to your *bad* habits. See how they fall into place? The *need* to keep active, for example, leads us to bite our nails, scratch, crack knuckles, etc. A physical or emotional *reward* tempts us to drink or over-eat. *Starter* stimulants, such as a cup of coffee or a specific time of day, urge us to reach for another cigarette. The color of a man's skin or the shape of his nose may stimulate in us a specific response toward that person. In other people, the very stimulus of their personality causes us to be angry, loving, or indifferent.

The *repetition* involved in holding a fork wrong when we eat, using bad grammar or profanity, or dressing sloppily, causes the habit to become more and more deeply entrenched in our minds until finally it is practically impossible to break. Wouldn't it be nice to have some good creative habits that were equally difficult to break? It will take some effort and time—but you *can* have them!

First of all, get into the habit of *thinking!* Don't allow your mind to wander aimlessly to the tunes of singing commercials, the padding of trivia, or the hopelessness of the past. Satisfy your needs with useful, constructive thoughts. Use your creative power tools well and often.

Get into the habit of thinking like the other guy. Anticipate his needs and desires, whether he be your employer, customer, or youngster.

A company's employees weren't responding to a campaign to submit cost-saving suggestions until one alert executive started "thinking like the troops" and came up with an idea for an enticing prize. The person who came up with the best "suggestion of the month" was entitled to use, for 30 days, a coveted parking space right next to that of the company president. Submissions of money-saving ideas increased more than 40 percent. His ENORMOUS ENLARGER technique led to magnifying the prize in the eyes of his employees.

Get into the habit of thinking of ways to make your money grow. Look for a money-making opportunity in everything that happens to and around you.

Julian Adler, a Tennessee realtor, developed a novel money-making scheme by using his COMPACT REDUCER power tool. Instead of selling land by the acre, he decided to sell by the square inch. He purchased one acre of land in each of the 50 states, subdivided them into one-inch parcels, drew up deeds for each square inch, and began selling them at 29¢ per inch. Each deed entitles the buyer to tenancy in common in one acre of dry, accessible acre of land—which means the buyer has free access to the entire area for camping, picniking, or parking. The majority of buyers had novelty gift-giving in mind, although others indicated they simply wanted property to leave in their wills. For each acre sold by the square inch, Julian could ultimately realize $1,829,065.60. His proceeds from all the acreage in all 50 states could total $90,-953,280!

Get into the habit of thinking "unorthodox." Reach for the "wild" solution—it may be the most practical in the long run.

The lawns of a cemetery had become something of an eyesore due to the heavy growth of weeds and underbrush, posing an expensive cleanup operation. A nearby farmer came up with a novel but inexpensive solution which the grateful operators quickly adopted. Eight hungry goats were released onto the grounds and allowed to eat their way among the tombstones. In a short time the lawns were neat and clean once again. Impressed by the animals' thorough job, owners of a nearby baseball stadium turned on their ALL-PURPOSE ADAPTOR and decided to use "Goat Power" to keep the grass trimmed on a steep embankment just beyond the outfield, thus saving themselves several hundred dollars each summer.

Get into the habit of thinking beyond the obvious. Search for the "real" problem, then attack it from many angles. Don't settle for the first solution you come up with.

Engineers for a large corporation were given the task of improving a thermometer. Orthodox thermometers were unsanitary, slow, hard to read, and breakable. Yet the thermometer was difficult to improve—in its present form. So the researchers, using their SYSTEMATIC SEARCHERS, began their search right at the source of the problem—temperature measurement. They attacked it there and consequently swung off in a completely different direction than they had previously tried. The result was an electronic "temperature taker" which provides an instant reading on a highly accurate meter via a device which is disposable after each reading. The finished product, a great stride forward in medicine, didn't even remotely resemble a thermometer.

Get into the habit of not accepting the "inevitable." Even if a thousand people have tried and failed to solve a problem, it's still available. Be the thousand and first to try!

For many years, fishermen in New England faced a common economic loss. About half to three-quarters of their fish were stored temporarily, as soon as caught, in barrels which were frequently replenished with fresh salt water to preserve as many fish as possible. The length of time they remained in the barrels, however, took its high toll among the fish. Finally, one creative fisherman used his PERFECT COMBINER device to hit upon a simple but effective method of reducing the "inevitable" death toll. He simply added an "enemy" fish into each barrel. As soon as he did this, it was as though he had electrified the fish: each sensed the enemy and wiggled and squirmed as hard as possible to stay alive. His percentage of live fish doubled—and his method was adopted by an entire industry.

Get into the habit of asking for assistance. The oftener you ask for help, the easier it becomes—and the more effective you become!

Jerzy Kosinski, a Polish author, knew practically no English when he came to America over a decade ago, yet in three years after his arrival he published his first book in English. To accomplish this, he had to ask for help—frequently. Since he knew no one in New York, and since he did most of his writing at night, there seemed to be no one he could ask for help. So he would call the telephone operator and say, "I'm a foreigner and I would like to read you a passage which I just wrote." He asked her if she would listen for a minute and tell him whether or not she could understand what he had written. Once the operators were assured he was not a crank, they would listen, then "play it back" to him, and comment on its clarity. In this way, he was constantly reassured that he was communicating clearly with his potential readers. He had used the SYNTHETIC SUBSTITUTER tool, substituting the operators for a larger audience.

Get into the habit of keeping your mind alive and active. When there's not much going on around you to tax your creative powers, pose hypothetical problems and brainstorm solutions to them.

Alvin Trent, a high school teacher, does this almost daily with his students, keeping them and himself thinking of solutions in quantity. Many times these are actual problems he or fellow teachers have faced (he often uses his IDEA RESURRECTOR for these). One of the most popular and effective such psuedo-problems was "How would you meet someone in an airport, railroad station, or subway, if you had never met him before or if you didn't know what he or she looks like?" In less than ten minutes, the youngsters came up with over a hundred ingenious suggestions.

Get into the habit of setting new goals and quotas for yourself. A philosopher once said, "Every dream come true had as its starting point, a dream." This applies here. Once you've achieved one goal, set new ones for yourself. Never be without one.

Mac McGuire was a jack-of-many-trades. In addition to his full-time job, he supplemented his income as a professional photographer, an artist, an amateur magician, and a writer of short stories, articles and TV scripts. His goal had long been to write a full-length book, but he had never quite gotten around to it. He realized, finally, that the reason for this boiled down to a simple fact—he simply hadn't developed any *sustained* writing habits. His other writing had been done as the spirit moved him, and his sudden bursts of writing would be followed by weeks of inactivity in this particular field. Using the MIGHTY MODIFIER device, he revised his daily schedule, and he set himself a goal in the form of a resolution: he would write at least one page a day, regardless of whatever else happened or how he felt. He made a sign which read TODAY'S QUOTA: ONE PAGE and taped it above his desk. In a little over a year he had completed his book. "Do you realize," he told a group of fellow writers, "that a page a day is 110,000 words a year? That's the equivalent of a full-length novel!" He's now working on his second book—a page a day.

Let's turn back to the pages of Chapter One and review the goals *you* have set for yourself. When these goals are met, the rewards will be great, both emotionally and physically. Keep reminding yourself that good creative habits are the key to these goals. Review them often. Type them on a piece of paper and keep them above the sun visor of your car or by your mirror, or any place where you can review them as you perform some daily task.

STARTER STIMULANTS

Starter stimulants are essential in forming habits, good or bad. A sunny day, for example, may stimulate the desire to play golf;

a party may stimulate the desire for a drink or two; a tense situation may stimulate the desire for a cigarette. Starter stimulants act as the first step in a chain reaction of habits. Put this chain reaction system to work for you in developing good habits. Make everything around you a starter stimulant for creativity. Be aware of their possibilities—and be prepared to act when they start tickling your habits.

Here's just a partial list of effective starter stimulants. Add to it.

words	pictures	sounds
taste	problems	accidents
pain	pleasure	money
fame	combinations	weather
color	misfortune	music
pressure	disasters	world events
expressions like "It can't be done"		the word "no"

Here are some examples of how other dynamic persons have made effective use of starter stimulants—the very kind that are available to *you:*

Accidents. An engineer who slipped in a tub and cracked his head on a water faucet may, as a result, have developed a whole new industry. After his painful accident, he began exploring ways of making bathtubs without protruding faucets, and finally came up with a practical and safe fixture. Water enters through a special aperture in the wall of the bath instead of through the conventional metal faucet. Manufacture of the new product will entail only slight modifications of present processes, and because of its simplicity, the purchase price is even lower than that of conventional tubs.

Danger. A soldier in Brisbane, Australia, was swimming some yards offshore when a large shark approached him. There was no time to call for help and he obviously couldn't outswim the creature, so he decided to use "scare tactics." He took a deep breath and dived straight at the shark. As he did so he blew out air and made bubbles, which apparently frightened the shark who immediately swam the other way. The soldier then wasted no time but swam to shore before he had a second opportunity to test his creative thinking!

Wastefulness. Paul Somers hated to see anything wasted, and when he read that the city of Seattle was going to replace 2,840 parking meter heads at the cost of some $175,000 in order that the meter rate could be raised, he was particularly disturbed. He asked for, and received, permission to tinker with one meter, and discovered a way to adjust them to the city's needs for one cent each.

Daydreams. Psychologists say that people who daydream frequently surpass others in creativity and resourcefulness. This was certainly true in the case of Sam Clarison who began dreaming of a treasure hunt after reading a magazine article on sea diamonds. A specialist in laying submarine pipe, Sam invented a machine for digging trenches in the floor of the ocean near the shoreline where rich diamond fields were located. In the first eight months of his operation, he grossed over 1.5 million dollars in rough diamonds.

The written word. Howard Jorell, a college journalism professor, has a constant need for information on a variety of topical subjects for his classroom and for articles and books which he writes. He realized that cramming desk drawers with random notes and clippings and making frequent trips to the library were disorganized and timewasting, so he developed a "system." Now, whenever he sees an article on a topic of interest, he clips it and places it in one of the rows of boxes lined up in his cellar, each labelled with the name of a general subject area. In these boxes he puts clippings, tear sheets, reprints, and his own scribbled notes, making the containers something of a personal memory bank.

Blank paper. Jean McManus finds, as do many writers, that one of the most creatively stimulating items is a blank piece of paper. "When I see one," she says, "I can hardly wait to start writing something on it!" For this reason, her home and office is filled with pads of paper, each placed at strategic spots—including her bedside. In the morning when she awakens, her first act is to jot down whatever comes to mind on the pad beside her. By mid-day, when most of the chores are done, she has scribbled down numerous notes and is well on the way to a productive, creative day.

Irritation. Bill Lane, accounts receivable manager, had tried his entire bag of tricks, pleadings, and threats on a delinquent account, but to no avail. "Why not send him a telegram?" asked one of his accountants. "It's against the law," Bill replied, then added hesitantly, "I think." Upon checking, he found that sending dunning telegrams is perfectly legal, so he tried one—with almost immediate results. Now he uses telegrams frequently, many times selecting the right time and place to hit the account with the greatest psychological effect (such as at home, just after dinner, or at the office just before lunch). His collections have improved greatly.

Enthusiasm. George North, a Boy Scout leader, knows that any group of people working on a problem together generate enthusiasm for carrying out their plans. A group of young boys is no exception. So he uses a method of preparing for campouts which generates enthusiasm and at the same time, teaches the scouts to plan ahead and to accept responsibility. Before each weekend outing, he calls the gang together and asks them, "What must we take with us for the weekend? Tell me; I'll write it down, and that's what we'll bring." Purposely, he brings only those things which the boys have listed. If no one mentions matches, there will be none; if they forget to list tents, blankets, etc., they do without those for the weekend, too. The boys enjoy being personally responsible for successful outings.

Suggestions. Beverly Taylor, a composer, relies on sounds of all kinds when she starts to write a tune. First she sits at the piano and lets her fingers run over the keys awhile. Keeping her RE-MOVABLE RE-ARRANGER always active, she tries dozens of combinations. She never knows in advance just what combinations of notes will attract her to a theme. Her fingers trip over the keyboard, starting and stopping, replaying the start of a tune. Then she goes outside, takes a walk and listens. Oftentimes the sound of a bird, a cricket, childrens' laughter, a squirrel, a train in the distance, a passing truck, or an overhead plane will start another combination of sounds within her mind—sounds which lead to a new tune or theme. She admits one of her most popular songs resulted from listening to a group of clucking hens as she strolled through a barnyard one day.

USE REPETITION TO STRENGTHEN
YOUR GOOD HABITS

An old Spanish proverb says, "Habits are at first cobwebs, then cables!" The more we repeat an act, the more it becomes second nature to us. If what we repeat is useful and creative, then we end up with a good habit. If it's a crutch, we have a bad habit. It's as simple as that.

Some habits are neither good nor bad; they are simply functional and necessary. For example: shaving, bathing, brushing teeth, getting dressed, washing dishes, mowing the lawn, driving a car, or walking. But they are habits and are deeply ingrained in us. Why not combine a creative action with each of these. In the process you'll turn the creative action into a habit, too.

Here's how it works for others. Think of ways to make it work for *you*.

Shaving. Don Foster, a salesman, makes it a point to add key words to his sales vocabulary daily. Each morning he posts above his mirror three words and their meanings. As he shaves, he reads the words, studies their meaning, and prepares short sales pitches using them. The method has helped make him one of the highest paid salesmen in his field.

Bathing. Werner Garth takes a five to ten minute shower every morning, during which time he plans his day in his mind, outlining the action he intends to take, the people he wishes to contact, meetings, and other items of business. "I've done this for so long," Werner, admits, "that my mind just seems to turn on the minute I step into the shower stall."

Walking. Mike Rodner, a dentist, after a month in the hospital with heart trouble began convalescing by walking. He would walk a little farther each day until he was able to walk five miles before breakfast. To make it more interesting, he walked a different route each day, seeing new sights and learning more about his city. In addition, he has taken up public speaking, and practices his speeches aloud as he walks. His health has improved immeasurably, and he now enjoys his new outlet as a public speaker.

Talking. "As long as we're talking, why not make it count for something?" That was the question Mark Townsend, an engineer, asked himself at a dinner party one evening. He was plagued with a business problem he'd been unable to solve and so he blurted out the problem to several men from an un-related industry. The men, though ignorant of the intricacies of the problem, took an interest in it. An informal brainstorm led to a practical solution, which the young engineer "polished"—and which resulted in a cost saving of nearly $10,000 a year to his company.

Getting dressed. Neil McCoy uses the ten minutes each day it takes him to get dressed to read a few pages from a book at the same time. "I try to keep a 'morning book' and an 'evening book' going," he said. "The morning book is always a positive, happy one—often a self-improvement book. The evening book may be anything from fiction to trade stuff. I get through several extra books every month this way."

Washing dishes. Rose Kaufman is a free-lance writer who has difficulty finding "thinking time" due to her large family. "So I chose the one time the family leaves me completely alone—when I'm doing the dishes. It's then that I get most of my ideas. I jot them down (soap suds and all) on a pad beside the sink. I can come up with several dozen good ideas a day this way."

Use time as a starter stimulant, too. Arrange to conduct many of your creative activities at specific times each day. Repetition of these activities will build strong creative habits.

PAY ATTENTION TO LITTLE THINGS— THEY'RE IMPORTANT

Throughout this book, we've stressed the importance of the many little things that make up a dynamic, creative personality. That's because it *is* the "little things" that count. Great ideas, unfortunately, don't descend from the heavens in a silver chariot driven by a triumphant, smiling muse. They are the results of dozens, hundreds, sometimes thousands of little bits and pieces of information, thoughts, and happenings carefully stored within your mind.

A tangible demonstration of the fantastic power of "little things" coupled with perseverance is this unusual incident:

Three Connecticut communities experienced a power failure that left them in total darkness for several hours. The cause was finally traced to *ants!* It was discovered that the insects had managed to chew their way through the base of an oak tree some 14 inches in diameter. The tree finally gave way and fell on the power lines, putting them out of commission. Experts estimated it had taken the ants over a year to complete their "lumber-jacking."

Make certain that the "little things" in *your* life are positive, not negative. Make every effort to replace bad habits with good creative ones. There are three dangerous habits which appear to plague most creative people:

> Idle talk
> Laziness
> Contempt for the work at hand

Learn to recognize, understand, and avoid them. They can reduce your effectiveness.

Avoid idle talk. Too often conversation becomes a substitute for creation—especially gossip, petty talk about the weather, or chatter for the sake of filling a void of silence. When *you* talk, have something to say.

Avoid laziness. We all have a touch of laziness in us, but it's important to keep it under control. Laziness is an energy-sapper and a dwindler, and it is all too easily rationalized. Avoid MENTAL CRUTCHES such as "I'm too depressed to work," "I'm upset today; I'll try again tomorrow," or "I'll just lay off for a few days and recharge my batteries." Get and keep the "busy" habit.

Avoid contempt for the work at hand. This is perhaps the most dangerous bad habit an idea person can allow himself to have. "Why should I lower myself to do this kind of trivial nonsense? I should be doing greater things!" You may find yourself asking at times. Your answer, of course, should be "Because it's there!" Recognize and accept the limitations of the job at hand, and decide that you're going to work within those limitations. Once you've done this, forget about them and tackle the job with all the creative ability at your command. Remember the old saying, "You cannot do any piece of work without learning something." There's a simple conclusion we can draw from this: the more you work— the more you learn!

GET THE SELF-CONFIDENCE HABIT

There are a lot of *do's* and *don'ts* in this book, and by putting them to use, you can accomplish a great many things. Providing, of course, you have confidence in your ability to accomplish a great many things. One of the crutches so many people use is "That may be good advice for the other fellow, but it just won't work for me. I'm not built that way!" That's all it is, though—a crutch.

Take a look at the case histories we've used throughout the book to illustrate points. Do you see any Supermen or Wonder Women here? There are no kings, emperors, presidents; no Olympic champions; no famous movie or TV stars—not a bona-fide genius in the lot! These are simply other people—like you or your friends or your co-workers or your family—people who had confidence in their ability and who used that ability to cope with everyday problems.

These people are not dynamic personalities in the sense that they will ever find their pictures on the cover of *Time* or their name on a Broadway marquee or their likeness in the Hall of Fame. But they *are* dynamic people. They are dynamic because they have learned how to tap the limitless source of creative power within them. They are dynamic because they have learned to *do something* with that power.

Now—what about *you?* You have all the equipment you need. You had it even before you picked up this book. You have all the time you need. Fortunately, you have the same 24-hour day with which to work, play, and live as does even the world's most dynamic personality.

Do you have all the self-confidence you need? If so, you're ready to go! If not, put your principles of dynamic habit-forming to work and get the confidence habit! Self-confidence is born of achievement—a total pattern of successful experiences; habit comes from repetition. So get yourself into the habit of accomplishing something creative every day. It needn't be a headline-grabbing, earth-shaking accomplishment. Most such accomplishments weren't achieved in a day, either. Your only requirement is that it should be a creative act. Consider each such act a step towards your development of a dynamic personality and you'll find the steps becoming more meaningful, more exciting.

As you do this, keep in mind the poet's words:

One seed at a time and the garden grows;
One drop at a time and the river flows;
One word at a time and the book is read;

One stroke at a time and the paint is spread;
One chip at a time and the statue's unveiled;
One step at a time and a mountain is scaled.
One thing at a time and that done well
Is the only sure way to succeed and excel.
You can write, you can paint, you can sculpt or climb:
You can do it by taking one step at a time.

One final word of warning. Once you start "turning on" your dynamic personality, you'll be hooked! You'll find the experience a lot like taking mind-expanding drugs—only far more satisfying and much more rewarding. So be prepared to stick with it. Never stop with solving just one problem creatively. Go on to the next—and the next—and the next. Don't be disturbed if the solution to one problem creates another; that's part of the game.

Stick with it! Thomas Edison once said that 75% of the world's failures wouldn't have failed at all if they'd only kept at what they were trying to do. He left us this thought:

Our greatest weakness lies in giving up. The most certain way to succeed is always to try just one more time.

How about it? Is that full life you want to live worth a little extra effort—that "one more time"?

You bet your dynamic personality it is!

INDEX